W.C. Fields & Me

W.C.Fields

&

Me

by Carlotta Monti with Cy Rice

Prentice-Hall, Inc., Englewood Cliffs, N.J.

Sixth printing. . . . . .July, 1971

ISBN 0-13-944454-8
Library of Congress Catalog Card Number: 72-143032
Printed in the United States of America T
Prentice-Hall International, Inc., London
Prentice-Hall of Australia, Pty. Ltd., Sydney
Prentice-Hall of Canada, Ltd., Toronto
Prentice-Hall of India Private Ltd., New Delhi
Prentice-Hall of Japan, Inc., Tokyo

I dedicate this book to myself, for the many years of loving service and kindness I willingly gave him.

Carlotta Monti

Introduction

IF nurtured by happy memories, the heart stays perpetually young compared with other components of the human body. It lags behind in obeying the dictates of the aging process. Certainly it will falter and die someday, but right up to the final moment of life, its beat can be quickened by treasured thoughts of love and devotion and ecstatically good times. My heart is that way today . . . responsive to the indelible fourteen years I lived with W.C. Fields.

Thirty-eight years have passed since I first laid eyes on him, yet it seems only last week. I feel that he has never left me. Sometimes I wake up during the middle of the night in the bed in which he died, and I sense his presence in the room.

As his mistress, I suffered the certain slings and arrows that irrevocably accompany that title. But I strengthened my mind against them, for I was not a kept woman as that word literally implies. At his invitation—without any bargaining, bartering, or promises—I moved in and lived with him. I never regretted doing so, for my only motive was love.

No one knew him better than I. Producers, directors, actors, and writers of superior intelligence may have thought otherwise, but they were wrong. I bedded down with him and gave him pleasure . . . I was his constant companion and confidante. My years with him ran into thousands of fun-filled, often tempestuous hours. When he died, my life abruptly changed. I went from a mansion to a furnished room, a boring job, and dull, routine living.

But oh, oh, oh, those fourteen years . . . !

Many have said that motion picture studios are cowardly, that they only follow trends, afraid to break the mold of past successes. But they pioneered with W. C. Fields.
His pictures contained none of the ingredients that were supposed to insure box-office success. There were no beautiful women, no torrid love scenes. Fields' movies were filled with cheating, thievery, the lowest of characters. The hero was a villain who never reformed—a likeable bad man. And Fields fitted the role perfectly: He was just playing himself.

People have complained that he was difficult to work with. Of course he was—most geniuses are. He was also difficult to live with.

They have said he was crochety, castigating, had a jaundiced eye, was larcenous, suspicious, shifty, erratic, frugal, and mercenary. I can only confirm these accusations. But he was also loveable, kind, sweet, generous, thoughtful, and gentlemanly.

Combining all these characteristics, you get a very mixed bag of a man. I can't deny that he was an anomaly.

To the public he had squinty, shifty eyes; a nose, of which it has been said that "if a bug crawled over the surface, pockmarked with a network of gulleys, canyons, and crevasses, it would prove an inescapable death trap to the insect," and a voice that was abrasive enough to scratch the purest of mountain air.

To me, his nose, for pure beauty, rivalled the perfect one of his friend, Jack Barrymore. His voice was the blending of tuneful sounds; and his eyes could cause a tingling of delight in my spine.

Prejudiced? Certainly—because he was my man and I loved him deeply.

He used to say, "Carlotta is fiery and unpredictable, but thoroughly wonderful and loyal." I think I was.

During the years I lived with him, I saved recordings, scribbled notes, and stored hundreds of incidents and anecdotes in my mind. I have attempted, with the help of a professional writer, Cy Rice, to translate them into a book.

I hope I have successfully rolled back the years.

Carlotta Monti
Hollywood, California

W.C. Fields & Me

One

MOST people start their day with breakfast. At five-thirty on that sad morning in 1932, I began mine with tears.

For three days and nights I had been deep in agonized mourning for a lost love—a famous professional wrestler known to the sporting world as "The Wonder Boy." He had recently stepped into the ring in Boston to discover his toughest battle would be an unscheduled one—and it would not be with his opponent. Just before the opening bell, he was served with a warrant for his arrest, charging him with having impregnated a girl in California.

They say that wrestling matches follow a script. On this particular night I'm sure that my man—he of the beautifully chiseled facial features and rippling muscles—didn't. He was seething. Within nine minutes, he had pinned his opponent twice.

His brother broke the news to me at my Hollywood apartment. His opening words were, "Jack's getting married."

Calmly, I asked for details. Then I said goodbye to the man who had almost become my brother-in-law and managed to prepare a lunch for my little sister, Eloise, to take to school.

After she left, I flopped down on my bed, beating my fists into the mattress.

How could this happen to me? I asked myself over and over again. I was the first girl Jack had ever had. Well, one thing was obvious: I hadn't been the last. Two years of courtship culminating in an understanding were gone, and with them, the thrill of being in love.

* * * * * * * * *

I dried my tears once again and wiggled into the tight grass skirt of a hula outfit that had been lent to me by the wardrobe department at Paramount. That studio had made arrangements to borrow me from RKO (to whom I was under contract) for the day; they were scheduled to pay me twenty-five dollars for posing for publicity stills with some male movie star—just who, no one had bothered to say.

My Italian-Mexican-Spanish ancestry (my real name was Montijo) was responsible for my light olive complexion. I weighed 120 pounds, my waist was twenty-four, my bust thirty-six, and I measured five-feet-six inches tall. For this Hawaiian motif, I had pinned flowers in my extremely long hair and let it flow down my back. Normally I wore it gathered into a big, black braid for a sort of coiled-serpent effect.

I managed to stifle the tears and patch up my face. When a girl is only twenty-four and wrinkle-free, the job is fairly simple.

The Depression was still at its depth, stocks were at 10% of their 1929 value; unemployment was on the rise, with fifteen million out of work; and Charles A. Lindbergh, Jr., the nineteen-month-old son of Colonel Charles A. Lindbergh, had been kidnapped. But these happenings seemed minimal compared with my own present crisis.

I taxied to Paramount where, on the lot, an assistant director said, "I'll introduce you to the man you're working with."

I wasn't even mildly curious as to who he was. The very word "man" repelled me. We took a shortcut through a crowded Cecil B. De Mille set, and made our way toward a little knot of people. I knew the star was somewhere in the center of the group, properly surrounded, "yes sirred" to death, and generally being fawned over.

As soon as a few people stepped aside to let us through, I recognized the face, the figure, and the silk hat and cane I had seen in his latest picture, *Million Dollar Legs*, in which he had more than held his own with comedians Jack Oakie, Andy Clyde, Ben Turpin, Hugh Herbert, and Billy Gilbert.

"Mr. Fields," the assistant director said, "this is Miss Monti, who will be doing the stills with you."

Instantly doffing his gray stovepipe hat, W.C. Fields placed it over his breast and bowed low before me. "It is a pleasure, my dusky beauty," he murmured.

I smiled, acknowledged the introduction, and stepped back to study this gentleman who sported an oversized poppy in his lapel. In 1932, the mumbling comic with the scratchy voice was blond, trim-figured, and handsome, with an unblemished complexion and bright blue eyes. Such a flattering portrait may seem incredible to those familiar with the movies he made during the 1940s, at which stage of his life his face resembled a relief map of some coal mining district, suffering from perpetually hard times. But when I first met Fields, the omnipresent martini had not as yet exacted its toll on his physiognomy.

He must have been thirty years my senior—but that was a mere triviality. He looked cute and cuddly. I wanted to mother him, smother him with attention, please him. My heart was beating slightly faster, but the cadence and rhythm were normal, and suddenly my damaged emotions were miraculously being repaired.

After shooting the stills, he gently took my arm in a boyishly bashful manner, his touch light and hesitant, and walked me to the gate. Several persons on the lot turned their heads in surprise. It wasn't studio protocol for a star to escort an unknown over those acres of concrete. But as I was to find out, W.C. Fields was the last man on earth to respect any form of protocol, diplomacy, or convention.

"One moment, my dear," he said, slowing his steps and disengaging his hand to toss away the long cigar he was smoking.

I remarked, "You didn't have to do that on my account, Mr. Fields."

His eyes swept my hula skirt. "It was a matter of precaution," he replied. "I didn't want to start a grass fire."

At the gate he pinched my cheek and said, "My, but you're a pretty one," and warned, "Be careful of marauders—they're behind every bush."

He tipped his hat, I smiled, and we walked in opposite directions. My feet dragged, reluctantly putting distance between us. I felt sure I would never see him again. I had been dying for him to ask for my telephone number.

Before I was out of hearing range I heard a man accost him: "You're looking fine, Bill!"

The answer returned in a voice that seemed to tunnel through underground passages: "Haven't been sick a single day since I had tuberculosis as a boy. A steady diet of cigars and whiskey cured me."

For the first time in three nights I slept well.

The next day was Sunday. At midmorning, Gene Towne, a writer friend of mine, telephoned. "It's a beautiful day. I have to deliver some scripts to the Valley and I thought you might like to take a ride," he offered, mentioning he could pick me up at about three-thirty. I said I would enjoy it very much.

The San Fernando Valley is composed of 275,000 square miles of land adjacent to Hollywood, which is part of Los Angeles. This vast expanse is scorching hot in the summer and shivering cold in the winter—neither of which is ever admitted by its inhabitants. In 1932, the legions of real estate signs weren't blocking off the pastoral scenery, and along Ventura Boulevard, the main north-to-south artery leading to Santa

Barbara, real grass was still visible; the coming of commerce hadn't yet threatened its extinction, nor had the birth of smog filtered out the vivid coloring.

We reached Encino, turned on White Oak Avenue—a street of large estates—and drove through a pair of gateposts. Between groves of oranges, avocados, and some pomegranates, I could see a beautiful, secluded Spanish home, and as we approached it, a tennis court, swimming pool, and aviary. The ranch grounds must have covered five acres.

Gene parked the car in the driveway, got out and opened the door on my side. He acted somewhat nervous. "Come on in," he invited, leading me to the hand-carved front door. By now I was mildly curious as to who might live amid this peaceful magnificence.

Gene rang the doorbell. A servant admitted us. Looking past him into the cavernous interior of the house, I saw a familiar figure. It was W.C. Fields.

Immaculately groomed in a white pongee suit, he came forward and reached for my hand to kiss the back of it lightly. Then he promptly conducted me on a leisurely tour of the house. I could feel him stealing side glances at me, and I wondered if I shouldn't have been wearing something more exotic than a black suit with a white blouse, topped with a huge floppy hat.

I couldn't help commenting: "My, the rooms are so large, and you have so much space."

"They accommodate my phobia," he said, smiling.

"What phobia?"

"Claustrophobia. You know, morbid dread of being in closed rooms, narrow spaces. I like things big."

"Then I'm glad I wore my gigantic hat," I told him.

He grinned. "And I'm glad you have a sense of humor."

Our conversation was stilted, unsure. He seemed a little uneasy. Yet what impressed me most was his decidedly continental manner, his suaveness, politeness, affability. In the years I was to spend with him he would never fail to rise from a chair when a woman or a man entered the room—an act he later perfunctorily performed for a strange nurse who entered his sanitarium quarters as he was dying. He always held a chair for me, assisted me into a car, and executed a dozen other little amenities that delight a woman and seemed to come naturally to him.

No sooner had we finished touring the house than Fields' masseur, Bob Howard, arrived. This physical culture consultant of movie stars rubbed and pressed Fields' body with his skillful hands in a special exercise room, while Gene and I listened to radio music. Occasionally a butler appeared to ask if we cared for a drink. It seemed the same man never came twice.

"How many servants does Mr. Fields have?" I asked Gene.

My friend began counting on his fingers. "Nine, I believe," he said finally, adding, "Give or take a few he may hire or fire come tomorrow."

"Is he that difficult to please?"

Gene smiled. "You'll have to find out for yourself, Carlotta."

It was my turn to smile. "That day will never come."

Gene, Bob Howard and I stayed for dinner. I remember we had hors d'oeuvre served on a cart, after which we made our way to a buffet loaded with food. The men drank champagne, Fields had martinis, and I abstained. Afterward, Mr. Fields showed me around the grounds. All the props of romance were compressed into his acreage, including the scents of orange blossoms and night-blooming jasmine. Overhead a nearly full moon and bright stars seemed hung in the sky just for us.

Our chatting, sprinkled with much banter, was light and easy now. Rapport became excellent, and our respective senses of humor dovetailed. Lost for a moment in thought, I stopped walking and said, "I've been thinking . . . "

"About what?"

"What to call you."

"You mean like knave? Thief? Imposter?"

"No. Something having special meaning to me. I can't call you Mr. Fields, or William, or just plain Bill, or W.C." Suddenly a thought struck me, and I voiced it. "I know. I'll call you Woody [Wōō-dy, as in moody]."

"Does Woody fit me?"

I nodded.

"Why?"

"Well . . . " I hesitated, "It—it just fits because you're cute. Like—like a bear. I know that sounds silly."

"A bear can be very ferocious," he said. "Such as a grizzly, for example."

"I meant a teddy bear," I told him.

"Well, it's a bit illogical," he admitted, "but definitely not silly. In fact, the name is very dignified compared to Cuthbert J. Quincy."

I turned toward him, puzzled.

He cleared his throat. "Well, some years ago I was traveling on a single safari, hopelessly lost in the wildest of wild Africa. Zambezia, to be exact." He paused, and asked, "Have you ever been to Zambezia?"

"I don't even know where it is in Africa," I answered seriously.

"Good," he said. "Very good. This allows me much more latitude with the story, to say nothing of longitude." Again he cleared his throat, and continued. "I was deep in the heart of the rhinoceros country, living on the bark of the hucapukas tree. Unfortunately, rhino meat, which was plentiful, is inedible. It's tough as a broiled mother-in-law on the chef's night off."

Lighting a long cigar, he took a few puffs and went on: "I was slowly starving to death. The bark tasted awful to my bite. Then, quick as a flash, there was a stirring in a clump of kismus bushes, and out bounded a nattily dressed fellow carrying a tray of steaming hot corned beef sandwiches. A gusty tropical breeze wafted their odor toward me, and I was salivating.

" 'Give me one, sir,' I pleaded, rushing up to the stranger, tugging at his beard.

"He steadfastly refused. 'These are reserved for Cuthbert J. Quincy only,' he replied.

"I couldn't tear my eyes from the succulent sandwiches. In fact, they were glued to them, which made my orbs water. Mulling over the situation, I thought, 'I've never told a single lie in my entire life, but now is the time.' So I said, 'Kind sir, *I* am Cuthbert J. Quincy.'

"Pulling out my wallet, I handed it to him—after first, of course, counting the money. You can never be too trustful of bearded tourists. I instructed, 'Search through the pockets and you'll find my card of identification, definitely establishing me as the man you are seeking.'

"He set down the tray, resting it on the stump of a mocamedas tree. While he carefully examined the contents of my wallet—which mostly contained letters from my former agent, Billy Grady, wondering why I hadn't sent him his commission—I quickly ate all the sandwiches. Certainly it was not an honorable thing to do, but I justified the act as exemplifying the survival of the fittest."

"How were the sandwiches?" I inquired, going along with him.

"Not lean enough," he answered.

"Woody," I said, using his new nickname for the first time, "I think you're pulling my leg."

Sighing deeply, he concentrated his gaze on my limbs. "It would be a pleasure."

We walked slowly toward the house. Before going in, he kissed my cheek and said, "I'll call you tomorrow. Don't make any other dates."

Back at the house we listened to the radio, and Woody discussed his favorite entertainers—Jack Benny, Fred Allen,

Edgar Bergen, and the Walter Winchell program. During the ride home Gene tried to make conversation. I nodded absently a few times, disinclined to talk. Finally he gave up, speculating aloud, "Bill must have left you speechless."

Not at all, but I *was* in a rather helpless state. I know this was a quick transition from my recently lost man and my sacred vows to not let the four-letter word of affection creep into my life again, but Woody had left me in love.

My head was bursting with impressions and thoughts of him. Mental photos of him were flashing on and off, with the consistency of a neon sign. Beyond any doubt, he was going to invade my dreams that night.

TWO

THE next day Woody sent me a huge orchid-gardenia corsage and a chauffeur. The corsage carried me into a reverie of heavenly odors. The chauffeur, driving a new Lincoln roadster, deposited me at Fields' home. I was dressed in one of my many Chinese costumes, a three-quarter length white blouse with exquisite delicate black embroidery and black satin pants. On my feet were Oriental slippers.

Like every career-bent girl who had parts in movies, I was spending too much on clothes: about seventy-five dollars for each of the Chinese outfits, of which I owned six in assorted colors.

Woody's small eyes widened. He shook his head unbelievingly and complimented, "An Olympian goddess of beauty, if ever I saw one."

I laughed. Not at the gross exaggeration of the compliment that was tantamount to gallantry, but at his voice—a subdued snarl from a sandpapered larynx, delivering what in theater parlance is called "an aside."

Then he snapped his fingers. "Zounds! My good woman,"

he said, "at last it comes to me, my nickname for you. I'll call you Chinaman."

"That doesn't sound very tender or intimate. To the best of my knowledge, there are about 400 million Chinese."

"Quite true, my ripe little peach, quite true. Yet none of them possesses your preponderance of pulchritude."

Now, the name seemed quite satisfying.

Woody handed me a beautifully gift-wrapped package containing a makeup case. I kissed him lightly and gratefully. I had fingered this very case of black onyx cloisonné in Bullock's a few weeks before, gasping at the $500 price tag. It was really too extravagant, too handsome. It was meant for a movie star, and although I fervently hoped to become one, I wasn't a movie star yet.

On this first "date" we talked of many things—one of the topics being marriage. He asked if I had ever been wed, and I gave him the facts of a brief marriage I had made as a teenager —a mistake—but pointed out that all memories of it had faded. Then I asked about him.

"Well," he said slowly, "yes . . . and . . . no."

"Come on now, Woody. It has to be one or the other."

"Let me explain, my little bird of rare plumage."

I waited.

"I was married once," he admitted ruefully. "In San Francisco. I haven't seen her for many years. The great earthquake and fire of 1907 destroyed the marriage certificate. There's no legal proof."

The story sounded logical.

"Which proves," he added, "that all earthquakes can't be bad."

* * * * * * * * * *

For four straight days, I saw him on an almost 'round-the-clock basis—with the exception of the nights, when I went home. But in the evenings, he took me to dinner at Chasen's and other fine restaurants, ordering champagne and chateaubriand.

I seldom took a drink, my capacity being only one, but he made up for my lack of interest in alcohol by drinking much, eating sparingly.

His hands were beautiful, fingers shapely and graceful, strong from the years he spent on the stage, juggling anything from cigar boxes to whatever he could lift. And he could hardly keep these same nimble fingers off me. He wanted to hug and kiss me continually—and I will neither deny nor confirm my permissiveness.

Before he took me home on the fourth night, he began, "Chinaman . . ."

"Yes, Woody."

"We're pretty compatible, aren't we?" he said, reaching for my hand and softly caressing it.

"Very."

"Well," he said, "I'm not going to spread a handkerchief and get down on one knee before you, because my arthritis might hurt when I got up. But I have something important to ask."

My heart was pounding.

"Come live with me."

"But my career . . ." I was protesting faintly, no conviction in my voice.

"Keep it in mind," he advised. "Also keep in mind you will have a new career here, running my household. I'll give you an entire wing of the house for yourself." And then he uttered a short, meaningful sentence, the one every woman loves to hear: "I need you."

Right then and there I made a decision that I never regretted: My answer was yes.

* * * * * * * * * *

I had a great deal to do to prepare for my new life. First I had Eloise move in with another sister of ours named Suzie, then called a storage company to transport my belongings to the Fields ranch, and put my furniture in storage just in case our arrangement collapsed. Finally, a starry-eyed girl named Carlotta "Chinaman" Monti began living with the man she adored.

"You are never to leave me," he warned sternly, "or I'll have you drawn and quartered."

"I never will," I promised—a vow that was to be broken several times, only to have me swear it would never happen again.

Beginning with the first intimate night together when we consummated our love—I will not disclose the wonderful details except to comment briefly that it was ecstasy—I felt more intensively alive and responsive than any time before in my life, my mind quicker and honed to a fine sharpness, my energies keyed higher and stronger. Woody seemed starved for real love and affection, and I gave it to him in large quantities. During that first year I blossomed into full womanhood and I believe I grew prettier as my body ripened, responding to its physical needs. I was a woman wanted and needed, and according to my friends, it showed in my eyes. They seemed constantly shining with love and new discoveries and meanings of the vital force of living, and I was told they held a luminous quality.

Throughout the years, calm and stormy, that lay ahead, I often reminisced about our first meeting . . . how Gene Towne —Thank Heavens!—in the guise of a friend, had acted as matchmaker (a word I hate) and tricked me. Actually Fields, who was not the most popular man in the world where women were concerned, was far too proud to receive a turndown to his face. Gene had answered Woody's need for a modern version of a John Alden.

Soon after I started to live with Woody, Gene Fowler advised me, "Don't try to take anything away from him, Carlotta, just try to add something to his life."

* * * * * * * * *

My first disappointment—one that briefly undercut my memories of that initial night of non-wedded bliss—came on the very next morning. I have always loved to cook and honestly believe I'm really pretty fantastic in this department. I can turn out a gourmet meal as easily as a fry cook can produce a hamburger, handling Chinese, French, Italian and Spanish cuisines with consummate ease.

That first morning, then, I decided there was going to be a surprise awaiting Woody at breakfast after he washed and came downstairs. Fields' cook, a pretty, dark-skinned girl named Della, knew of my plans and was happy to step aside and let me be temporary majordomo of the kitchen. Singing an aria from *Carmen*, I went to work.

I was sure the meal I was preparing would be not only sumptuous, but eye-pleasing—one that would stir gastric juices in the most jaded appetite. On the mouth-watering menu: compote of fresh peaches and strawberries, shredded wheat (oven-warmed to restore freshness), baked French toast with marmalade sauce, rolled bacon strips, and the *pièce de resistance*, Eggs à la Rossini.*

When the repast was ready, I summoned Woody. He appeared in a crimson foulard robe over canary yellow, monogrammed pajamas. Deerskin slippers covered his feet.

As he came down the stairs, I admiringly examined my handiwork. The table was a masterpiece, the food tempting enough to make Mahatma Gandhi end one of his periodic fasts. I waited for the cry of surprise and joy, the words of praise that I was certain would tumble from Woody's lips.

All I heard as he entered the dining room was an untranslatable "Hummmph."

Frowning, he marched into the kitchen only to return carrying a small unidentifiable tin can and a bottle of champagne. Reaching into a pocket of his robe, he brought forth a can

* Take a large shirred egg dish, butter it, break in the eggs, place in the oven till barely set; then make a border of diced chicken livers encircling the eggs, cover the livers with Périgueux sauce and return to the oven until the eggs are set.

opener, used it to inexpertly saw open the can, and scraped something resembling dog food onto a solid gold-rimmed plate. Next, he spread honey on top of it, adroitly popped the champagne cork, sat down, bid me follow suit, and began wolfing that strange-looking food, washing it down with huge gulps of the bubbling wine.

"Woody!" I cried, my spirits crushed, "Whatever is that you're eating?"

He swallowed and looked up. "Scrapple, my dear," he enlightened. "Philadelphia scrapple."

"What's it made of?" I asked.

"It's made by boiling together scraps of meat, mostly pork, with chopped herbs and flour or Indian meal. Comes out like mush. It can be heated."

"Is it expensive?" I wanted to know, positive he must have had it specially imported.

"Five cents a can."

I staggered into a chair, unable to eat a bite, managing only a few gulps of black coffee to lift my sinking spirits.

"Care for some scrapple, my dear?" he offered.

Shaking my head, I began silently crying into a Belgian linen napkin. Then I jumped up, knocking the chair over, and ran up the stairs to the bedroom Woody had given me, neglecting to close the door. From downstairs I heard the butler ask Woody, "Is the young lady ill, sir?"

"It's nothing to be gravely alarmed about," the master of the manse replied. "Just a recurrent attack of Osteocopia, a disease rampant among savage-tusked wild boars whose habitat is the Isle of Flushdown."

Suddenly my tears stopped, and I began laughing uncontrollably. Woody heard me and called, "Is anything wrong, my dear?"

"Decidedly," I shouted down. "There's a wild boar in my bed."

He shouted back, "Is he from the Isle of Flushdown?"

"Yes, yes, yes! Can you save me?" I cried desperately.

I heard him running up the stairs, trumpeting, "Have no fear. I will confront the demoniacal monster and tear him tusk from tusk." With that, he charged into the room and jumped onto the bed beside me.

It was my Woody who turned out to be the demoniacal monster—but a very kind one, I must say. Later, when we were dressing, I dubbed him my "Knight in Shining Pajamas."

"Who rescued his damsel in distress," he added.

"Just like St. George who slew the mean, frightening dragon."

"Not exactly," he mused. "I had a lot more fun than old St. George ever did."

* * * * * * * * * *

At the beginning of my life with W.C. Fields I wouldn't have won any popularity contest if his friends did the voting. Some of them were openly rude, insinuating or even directly accusing that my affection had a single objective: to lay my hands on the W.C. Fields fortune. As Woody himself said, "If any unmarried woman loses her equilibrium, she should manage to fall on a millionaire."

Voices carried far in the house, and the fact that I was in the kitchen with the door half open helped me to overhear one particular discussion.

The writer, Gene Fowler, was defending me. "Ridiculous," he scoffed at the statement that I was a common golddigger. "No one could get a dollar away from that old skinflint—even with a gun."

Gregory La Cava, the director, spoke up. He was a man with whom I was constantly at odds. "I know at least five women Bill's given costly jewelry to, and they weren't armed."

"Maybe not," Fowler retorted, "but Uncle Claude must have been. I know he got all of it back—every single stone. He merely waited until the trinkets increased in value."

This, I was to discover, was true. Two women had even sued

Woody unsuccessfully for breach-of-promise. He had been changing girlfriends every seven years, a habit he claimed to have picked up from broken mirrors.

Among his friends—members of the regular drop-in club who came over for swimming, tennis, pool playing, croquet, table tennis, drinking, conversation, dinner, or what have you —Gregory La Cava was the villain. He started calling me a "dirty dago."

But Fields took umbrage at his slurs. "Just what do you think *you* are, you dago bastard?" Woody retaliated. "One of those saints your countrymen worship and whose statue they stick in their backyards?"

"Oh, there are different kinds of dagos," La Cava insisted.

"There certainly are," Woody agreed, "I know Italian history and the island *your* ancestors came from."

They would pick at each other, spoiling for a fight, no matter how inconsequential the subject for warfare might be. La Cava often deliberately asked for rare brandy or champagne of a certain vintage hard to obtain and if Fields failed to have it in stock, would speak of the inadequacies of his wine cellar.

The two of them would go 'round and 'round like this before burying their differences at the bottom of a cocktail shaker. Despite the fact that Woody often professed hatred for La Cava, he openly admitted, "He's the best director in the business."

Actually, Woody held no resentment toward any race, color, or creed. But for want of anything better to say, he mentioned to La Cava, "What do you want to work for all those Jews over at Universal for?"

"Whom do you have in mind?" La Cava asked.

Woody supplied two names.

La Cava laughed, "That shows how much you know," he said. "Neither one is a Jew."

"They're the worst kind," Woody returned, thus creating a joke that was to be copied many times.

Among Fields' intimates, John Barrymore was suspicious of me at first, but later, when he realized my feelings for Woody, we became good friends. Other regular frequenters at the house were Billy Grady—Fields' former agent from New York, later to become casting director at Metro-Goldwyn-Mayer; Bill LeBaron, the producer; Sam Hardy, Broadway stage comic; Charley Beyer, Fields' Hollywood agent; director Leo McCarey; producer Eddie Sutherland; writer Bill Morrow; restauranteur Dave Chasen; director Paul Jones; artist John Decker, who painted portraits of film personalities; the great Will Rogers; and Woody's costar in *You Can't Cheat an Honest Man*, Edgar Bergen.

I did little talking when this distinguished cliqué gathered. Instead, I listened and learned much. Witticisms were omnipresent, along with brilliant sarcasm, serious opinions, leg-pulling, tongue-in-cheek, double entendres, and above all, extensive use of a vocabulary which increased my own.

Commenting on these soirées, Edgar Bergen, himself an intelligent man, said, "I say very little; I just listen and learn."

I soaked up much knowledge from this brilliant ring of friends, and although mere fragments rubbed off on me, I felt like I was taking a crash course at a university.

Most of these friends called Fields "Uncle Willie" or "Uncle Claude," and a few, "Bill." Cornering John Decker, I asked him about the "Uncle" bit.

"Because he's avuncular," the artist said.

I still didn't understand.

"Because," Decker explained, "he looks like everybody's uncle—although he particularly reminds me of an unclaimed, befuddled uncle who got lost in a brewery."

After a number of years La Cava had learned for a fact that, with the exception of a few presents, Woody had given me only twenty-five to fifty dollars weekly for personal use. But even then he was still skeptical of my motives.

"I don't trust her," he said. "She's far too beautiful to hang around that drunken buzzard unless she wants something from him. What can she do for him anyway?"

As usual, my loyal army of one—namely, Gene Fowler—came to my defense. "Carlotta runs the household, does the marketing, helps his secretary with her duties, sews his buttons, mends his socks, and performs perhaps the hardest job of all—mixing his martinis."

"What's so tough about mixing his drinks?" La Cava demanded.

"You know Uncle Claude's capacity," Fowler pointed out. "It's a full-time job."

"Bah!" La Cava snorted. "That old reprobate would drink a cup of hemlock if it had an olive in it."

Woody and Fowler had some wonderful tongue-in-cheek discussions. They understood each other's great talents and had deep mutual respect. I used to jot down on a pad some of the dialogue that flowed freely between the two. Woody was always thinking up and trying out gags, and I'd attempt to keep pace with my pencil.

If I didn't laugh, he'd say aloud to no one in particular, "The Chinaman doesn't get it, so tear it up." And I would.

On really warm days, Woody might take a swim—if you could call it a swim, his paddling around a bit. But he excelled in one department of aquatics: floating. He looked neat and trim, and very buoyant, drifting on his back, but in later years, after heeding the advice of someone who convinced him that the combination of whiskey and milk was health-giving, he gained weight and floated around with the mound of stomach poking out of the water and his cigar belching smoke, making me think of a small tanker coming in for a berth.

Gene Fowler had once discussed doing a biography of John Barrymore to be titled *Goodnight Sweet Prince*, and one day, while standing waist-high in the pool, he speculated, "Some day I'll write your life story, Uncle Claude."

"While I'm living?"

"Of course not—posthumously. Were you ever known to follow a script? I don't want you blue-pencilling my work."

"When I die," Woody said, "I want you to take all my scrapbooks."

Fowler said that he would. Then Woody abruptly changed the subject. "Ah, you writers of books aren't so bad. You've some originality. But the screen writers! Impossible! They're sheep with no sense of reality."

"What are you referring to?" Fowler asked.

"Westerns," Woody replied, and, warming up to the subject, "I know the horses can't get killed. They're protected by the "cruelty-to-animals" code. But did you ever consider that with all those Indians twanging the bowstrings, and arrows flying around, how come one—just one—never lodged in the ass of an early settler? It could happen if someone made comic Westerns. Comedies are more honest.

"And those old towns—the men milling about the streets in great numbers. Some come flying through swinging saloon doors, booted in the rear by bouncers. Others stand around waiting for a shooting showdown in the center of dusty Main Street. Now, where are all the women? How many do you see? Only dance hall girls. The women in the town can't all be home baking cakes or washing the crud from their husbands' long underwear."

Fowler sighed and shifted the conversation to another topic. "Uncle Claude, if you ever get to Catalina, visit the aviary. There's an ugly bird there from Asia that sounds just like you."

"I'll go," Woody said, "and I'll take Loyd Wright along." (Wright was his attorney.)

"Why take Loyd?"

"Maybe we can sue," Fields replied. "Dratted comics have been stealing from me and imitating me for years. Now a bird is doing it. I'll tar and feather that accursed imitator." And, as an afterthought, he added, "Come to think of it, I won't have to bring the feathers."

"Thanks for the swim and drinks, Uncle Claude," Fowler said, "I've got to get back to work." He started for the house.

"Listen, Gene," Woody halted him. "If I give you a great, original plot as a gift, can you use it?"

"You know I don't write fiction."

"I'll give it to you, anyway," Fields persisted, as Fowler returned to sit down. "This is real realism. A man had a dog. Dogs and weather are made for the reading public, so you can't miss having a bestseller."

"Get on with the plot," Fowler urged.

Chewing reflectively on a toothpick, Woody tilted his chair back and elevated his bare feet to the poolside tabletop. "Well, this man with the dog educated him. Every day he gave the mutt talking lessons, and the first thing you know, the dog can speak and he's got a vocabulary of about a hundred words— which is fifty more than any of my scenario writers.

"The dog owner gets himself a theatrical agent, has him audition the animal, and the ten percenter is ecstatic. He has no trouble booking the act into the London Palladium. It's a Command Performance, and the Queen is sitting in the Royal Box.

"With much fanfare and an orchestral accompaniment, the curtain rises, and there is this talented animal sitting on a huge velvet pillow, while his master stands alongside.

"The audience applauds, and then the house becomes very still. The act has been well rehearsed and calls for the canine to recite the words to *God Save the King* in a British accent. The owner signals to the dog to begin. The animal growls a few times clearing his throat, and in a loud, clear voice come the words:

" 'Screw the entire British Empire!' "

Fowler stood up. "Uncle Claude, I'd advise you to stick to acting," he mumbled, and headed for the house.

Woody saw me scribbling furiously. "And make a note, Miss Monti," he said, "that I'm to stick to acting."

It was bad enough that La Cava was unrelentingly suspicious of my sincerity. But Fields harbored a deep distrust of any member of the human race, and when I first moved in with him, that included me. He would purposely leave sums of money in conspicuous places around the house, thinking it might tempt me. Once I saw a pile of money on a coffee table. Counting it, I noted there was $365. Feeling impish, I added five dollars of my own money, but he made no mention of the increase.

The supreme test, though, came on the day he summoned me to his office, which had been converted from a master bedroom.

"My little passion flower," he began, "I have an errand for you. I want you to go to the Security First National Bank in Hollywood and make a withdrawal for me."

"Of course, Woody," I said, only too happy to carry out his wishes.

He mentioned that he had telephoned the bank and completed all the necessary arrangements—and then he handed me a withdrawal slip. I looked at it and gasped.

"There must be some mistake."

"No mistake."

"But—but this—this is for $50,000!"

"Exactly, my little bird."

Stunned, I said, "You want me to go down to a bank, withdraw $50,000, and bring the money back to you?"

"Those are my intentions."

It was unbelievable. "But why so much money?" I blurted out, unthinkingly, knowing he wouldn't tell me the truth.

He didn't: "I need a couple of pairs of shoes shined and the boy at the stand has gone up in his price."

Thoughts of carrying that large sum of money began to petrify me. "Listen," I said, "Somebody can hit me over the head, take the money, and you'll say I stole it!"

"Just show me the bump and you're in the clear," he answered.

I went straight to the garage, climbed into one of his cars, and drove to the bank. The manager was expecting me. He asked no questions except for identification, and then just ushered me into the vault and counted out $50,000. As I had brought no suitcase or briefcase, one of the tellers used wrapping paper to convert the money into a neat brown package.

"Be careful," the banker warned.

His words frayed my nerves. I was shaking as I came out into the warm sunshine. Each person I passed on my way to the parking lot resembled Dillinger, Bonnie, or Clyde. Everyone's eyes seemed fastened on my package. I clutched the money tightly and kept glancing over my shoulder to see who was following me. Then I reached a decision: It was much too dangerous for me to drive alone and unprotected. Maybe my reaction came from seeing too many gangster movies, but I was dead certain some black limousine would force me to the curb, and a blunt instrument would come crushing down on my skull.

So I hailed a taxicab. Woody's chauffeur could pick up the car.

In the meantime, unbeknownst to me, Woody had called his agent, Charley Beyer. He was continually driving Beyer crazy, sending him on foolish errands and rousing him at all hours of the night. Nevertheless, Beyer had found it well worth putting up with his profitable client's idiosyncrasies.

"Drop everything, Charley," he now ordered, "and get right to the airport!"

"I'm not going on any trip, Bill," Beyer reminded him.

"Of course you're not," Woody stormed. "But that Mexican bitch, Carlotta, is. She just stole $50,000 from me and is trying to skip the country. Check all planes going south of the border."

"Why not call the police?" Beyer inquired.

"I don't want any bad publicity."

"But—but, Bill, I—I . . ."

"Get moving, Charley," Woody cut him off, "or I swear by

all the gods in the heavens I'll knock you down to five percent in the next film."

"I'm on my way, Bill," Beyer gulped, hanging up.

I arrived back at the ranch without incident, though rather shaken from the experience and with a splitting headache. Woody didn't see the cab drive away. I located him, thrust the money package into his hand, and started for my bedroom.

His voice crackled: "Just a moment, my good woman!"

Motioning me to follow, he went into the dining room, and opening the package, laid the currency in neat stacks on the table. Slowly he counted. Finished, he turned to me muttering enigmatically, "Aha—just as I suspected."

He stared at me accusingly.

"What's wrong, Woody?"

Pointing a forefinger at me and propelling it to within an inch of my nose, he ranted, "I'll tell you what's wrong. Some of the money is missing."

Oh no, I thought, Oh no, oh no, oh no—and I began silently praying.

"The missing amount is $6.50," he announced.

I couldn't believe my ears. Rapidly I explained my fears of safety to him and how I felt reasonably secure in a taxi and that the ride cost $5.45 and the rest was a tip.

"Chinaman," he sternly admonished, "you're a goddam philanthropist with my money. Besides, you overtipped."

For the next ten minutes he lectured on frugality and intimated that I was a spendthrift.

I said nothing. I just reached into my bag, counted out six one-dollar bills, plus fifty cents in change, and handed the money to him. Nodding curtly, he folded the money into his wallet.

I took two aspirin, and found them ineffectual. Then I made myself my very first martini, and discovered it had real medicinal value.

The next day something terrible happened to Woody that

almost seemed to be retribution, at first, but I really don't believe that people are paid back for wrongdoings, and of all persons, I didn't want the man I loved to learn a lesson the painful way.

Since nearly every room in the house contained a well-stocked portable bar, Woody hardly ever found himself where he couldn't stretch his arms in any direction and have his fingers touch a bottle. After mixing a martini in the master bedroom he, for some reason, decided to carry it down the staircase. On the way, his foot slipped and he bounced all the way to the bottom.

I heard the racket and came running. "Woody, why didn't you reach out and grab the railing? You could have braced yourself and prevented the fall."

From a sitting position on the first step, he triumphantly lifted the glass he still held in his hand. "Look!" he exclaimed despite the pain, "Not a drop spilled! Why, if I'd reached for the railing, I'd have lost the entire drink."

His extraordinary sense of balance, acquired during his juggling days, had prevailed. Well, he may have saved the drink—there was no argument on that point—but he had broken his coccyx, which proved to be exceedingly painful.

Three

OODY'S broken coccyx gave him particular grief because it brought him into necessary contact with members of the medical profession—whom he detested. Fifteen dollars was always Woody's top price for a doctor's visit, and he would quibble until a medico agreed to come for that set figure. I generally had to do the dickering. "I ought to move to China," he would say, "because there a doctor doesn't get paid while you're sick, only when you're well."

I'll always remember the time Woody sent for a doctor when he was constipated. After a lengthy examination, the doctor diagnosed, "Mr. Fields, you have a bowel obstruction."

"Use some dynamite and blow it out," Woody advised.

I cut into the conversation. "I think sauerkraut juice will cure him."

"Goddam it, Chinaman!" Woody reprimanded. "Keep your mouth shut! What do you think I'm paying this dissector of the human body fifteen dollars for?" He addressed the doctor, "What's your advice?"

The doctor replied, "I hate to admit it, but the lady is right. Sauerkraut juice should solve the problem."

And so it did, but instead of thanking me, Woody bawled me out. "If you had spoken up sooner, you'd have saved me fifteen dollars."

Another time, when he had a terrific cold, I advised him to drink a certain kind of tea that grew wild in California and would cause him to perspire.

"If I listened to you," he said, "I'd be dead in two weeks."

His doctor prescribed the same tea. Woody didn't thank me this time either. Instead, he said, "You ought to be arrested for practicing without a license, you meddlesome witch."

* * * * * * * * *

This time his recuperation was slow, and Woody was depressed. His sleep barely added up to two hours each night, and I, accompanied by his ever-present liquor, was continually at his side.

"I wonder which means more to you," I mentioned, starved for a compliment, "the drinks or me."

"Each has its position of relative importance in the household," he answered.

It was during this lengthy period of convalescence that Woody went on a reminiscing jag, dredging up his early life to acquaint me with where he had been before we met. He was truly a graduate of the College of Hard Knocks, most of them literally centering around his nose.

For some reason—perhaps because of his manner, his speech, his gestures—Woody was continually being set upon by bullies. His nose was always the target for attacks. Older kids seemed to sense that he was not one of their tribe, a misfit of sorts, and often mobs of them pursued him, emitting blood-curdling yells, bent on mayhem. Either he couldn't duck quickly enough or never learned to block a punch—I wasn't sure which. Early in life, long before drinking imposed the red-and-blue network of veins and lumpiness that was to make his proboscis a famous trademark, the Fields nose was already ungainly and spreading.

According to Andrew L. Stone, who directed Woody in his final screen appearance, *Sensations of 1945*, that protuberance was an object of great distaste to the makeup man, a gentleman of sensitivity. This man, in order to construct a plaster cast of the nose that would be worn by others in a skit, had to touch it. "It feels like a sponge," he muttered, shuddering. "Gives me the shivers," he went on to say, "I don't think it belongs on a human."

Except when he had to blow it or when it became painfully sunburned, I don't think Woody was acutely conscious of his nose—at least not to the point of allowing its size or shape to bother him. Should his friends joke about it in his presence, he was even mildly amused. "George Washington had a big nose," he reminded, "and he was the father of an entire country."

Cornering John Barrymore, whose perfectly-chiseled features earned him the nickname of "The Great Profile," Woody speculated, "If I had your nose and you had mine, our lives would be entirely different."

Barrymore thought this over while unconsciously stroking the side of his beautiful nose, and said thoughtfully, "I'd be a comic and getting a lot of laughs."

"Right," Woody concurred, "and I'd be getting a lot of women."

"You want to trade?" Barrymore asked.

"Why, no, unhesitatingly no," Woody drawled, "I'd be doing too much flitting hither and yon." And fixing his squinty eyes on me, he paid my vanity the supreme compliment. "I have one woman now, and the supply is sufficient."

* * * * * * * * *

Woody's father was an Englishman by the name of James Dukinfield. "He was a cockney, a London cockney," he recalled, "who somehow got over to this country. He reached Philadelphia, where there was little to do after dark, so he got married."

According to the man who ought to know, James Dukinfield of London married Kate Felton of the Germantown District. "Kate was a neighbor's daughter," Woody remembered. "It was a marriage of convenience, as my father had a blister on his big toe and couldn't travel very far to find a girl."

Named William Claude, Woody was born on April 9, 1879. The family had a difficult time scratching out a living, as young Claude's father hawked vegetables and fruit from a horse-drawn wagon.

Woody's hair was a light blond, earning him the nickname of Whitey. Whitey was acceptable enough to him, but his parents thought otherwise. To them he was Claude, a name the boy despised. He made a number of abortive attempts to get his father to change it legally to Whitey. For his efforts, he got so many cuffs on the head with the back of his father's hand that he said he often wondered what the other side of the hand looked like.

When telling me about it, he said, "I should have known better in those early days than to try to accomplish anything legally." Later, of course, for professional reasons, he changed his name to W.C. Fields.

Other Dukinfield children followed the birth of William Claude: sons Walter and Le Roy, and daughters Adele and Elsie Mae. "None of them," Woody chuckled, "inherited my beauty."

Once he got away, Woody experienced no nostalgia for the place of his birth. "Philadelphia," he reminisced, "was a gay, lighthearted town. Anyone found smiling after the curfew rang was liable to be arrested. If a woman dropped her glove on a street, she might be hauled before a judge for stripteasing. The city had so many reformers, they tried reforming each other."

The elder Dukinfield took him along on vegetable selling wagon tours and on any day when his own cockney accent was laid low by laryngitis, he encouraged the boy to use his vocal chords for hawking. This suited Woody's fancy. It was an escape from the norm—and he was on stage. Often his inventive mind prompted him to call out startlingly new produce such as "roundmelons, appleheimers, beans à la mode, finklebagas," and many others which drew droves of curious housewives to the wagon. For his ingenuity, he received the customary cuffing around the head.

For a man who barely flirted with an education, he spoke grammatically, conjugated his swear verbs perfectly, and had a photographic (not to mention scheming) mind. He stored everything he read in the library of his mind, kept it well dusted, and knew precisely which shelf it occupied. Many times he amazed me and his friends by quoting long passages verbatim after a single scanning. Though he delved into the dictionary and *Roget's Thesaurus*, he cared little if he used a word improperly by definition; if he fancied it, he sneaked it into a sentence nevertheless.

When I asked how much formal education he had had, he replied, "Second grade."

"Did you have to quit to make a living?"

"Hell, no," he replied. "For raping my teacher."

One dark night when he was nine or ten years old, he simply walked away from the house, never to return. His new homes (of which there were many) consisted of holes in the ground, caves, abandoned buildings, tumbledown wooden shacks, basements with stoves, and other such abodes. He doubts if his absence was reported to the authorities.

He led a helter-skelter, hand-to-mouth existence and was careless in his ways. Woody admitted having been jailed a number of times, but stoutly maintained his lockups were only for petty crimes hardly worth mentioning, such as "vagrancy, larceny, and murder." No jailhouse ever had a record of any W.C. Dukinfield as a lodger, probably due to the many aliases he used, in addition to the fact that no nationwide system of fingerprinting was then in effect.

He didn't mind these incarcerations too much—the food was far better than what he normally put into his mouth. Forays for edibles led him to saloons for free lunches. In any establishment where he felt management was becoming suspicious of his freeloading, he would first buy a ginger ale or root beer for a nickel, and then feel obliged to plow his way through copious helpings of bologna, liverwurst, and cheese. His patronage was intermittently discouraged by the toe of a pointed shoe.

After a year of bumming around and a few half-hearted attempts at holding down jobs, Woody moved in with his widowed grandmother. I never heard him speak very much about this relative except for a couple of passing remarks: "She was a very peculiar woman. She objected to children stealing for a living." And, "She was blindly trusting; she got me a job as cash boy in a department store."

Of the job, he remarked, "It was easy and gave me a feeling of security, but the trouble was the store had too many entrances and exits. I kept going out and not wanting to come back in again."

During much of his spare time—which added up to many hours nightly and daily—he practiced juggling. While working for his father as a fruit and vegetable peddler, he had begun by tossing apples and oranges into the air. He exhibited extraordinary skill for one so young. He rarely dropped a piece of fruit—once a grapefruit, something too large for his childish hands. This in itself was not too tragic, except that his father saw it hit the ground, and his career as a juggler was thus temporarily stymied.

Now, unhalted and uninhibited, he threw everything he could lift into the air—from tennis balls that sailed over fences to miscellaneous objects he picked up in the city dump after studiously avoiding the large rats foraging about.

His grandmother, a woman of wisdom to match her years, came to the realization that this was no ordinary boy and was positive that under no circumstances would he ever succumb to the conventional standards or dictates of society.

They parted firm friends.

Later, poolrooms were to become his classrooms, where he studied the "pool sharks" of the day.

His entrance into a pool hall—the most fortunate thing that ever happened to him—was by chance. Originally he did not go in to play the game, but because he saw a glowing hot stove from the window and he was freezing. Before the day's end he had a job racking up balls and sweeping the joint. Occasionally he found a coin on the floor.

He later contended that during some nights he still heard ghostly voices from his past calling, "Rack 'em up, boy!"

As a hustler he was magnificent. While practicing, he couldn't seem to make a shot even if the ball stood an inch from a pocket, but the moment a sucker challenged him, he started running the table. It wasn't unusual for a stranger to wander into the parlor and observe a practicing Woody shaking so badly from palsy— or what he called "quivermylitis"—that he missed the cue ball. He appeared to be ripe for the plucking. But after the stakes were decided and the game got under way, the shaking mysteriously abated. As Woody the hustler ran out ball after ball, he could be heard to mutter, "May have a recurrent attack any minute." If he did have one, it always came just after the bets were settled.

He once won a sizeable wager playing with the wrong end of the cue. And another time, after losing a match, he reversed the score by "accidentally" dropping the cue ball on the foot of his opponent who had a sore bunion.

"I missed my calling," he told me after relating the story years later, "I should have been a bombardier in World War II."

As a house player he was a whiz, but he often drove the pool hall owner up the wall by injecting bits of hilarious comedy that made him come dangerously close to losing matches. Later he expanded on these to incorporate them into musical comedy skits, and they eventually found themselves in the movies. His cue on these occasions was a crooked staff, and with it he often ripped the cloth from the table, chalked his finger by mistake, and pulling back for a shot, jammed the tip of the cue forward against the underside of the table.

After he became wealthy in California, he always installed a pool table in his house, which he used for recreation, therapy and gambling. He described it as "a beautiful sight for sore eyes, this greensward." I'll never forget the morning I rose early, went downstairs, and saw him stretched out upon the pool table in his pajamas. I first thought he had suffered a stroke. After my scream awakened him, he yawned and said sleepily, "A pool table was one of my early beds, my dear, and all of us unconsciously revert to our childhood."

He had not slept in a real bed from the time he ran away from home until he was seventeen-years old. Two years before I gave him one, he had had a door removed from a room, padded the room with hay, and over the hay he packed sacks. "Most comfortable bed I ever slept in," he often recalled. He slept in freight trains, on pool tables, in fields, on concrete floors near basement stoves, crammed into telephone booths where he either stood up or wedged, folded up, into the bottom.

Perhaps the most gratifying early job he held was on a horse-drawn ice wagon, riding with his boss who drove it in the wee hours of the morning in Philadelphia. Night driving was necessary because it was summer and the cool of darkness preserved the ice longer. The moment the hot sun rose, the stock diminished, melting into the streets.

Woody and his boss enjoyed instant rapport. Neither was ever in a hurry, and the same mood enveloped the pokey old horse, the kind of animal you see wearing a hat in an old cartoon.

Woody handled the smaller cakes of ice, those under fifty pounds. Toward the end of the run, when the sun began its evaporation, he often sat on a small cake to keep cool, or shaved off some chunks which he sucked on, later contending, "That's when I developed an overwhelming hatred for drinking water."

Dogs took a different attitude toward Woody than his iceman employer did. "For a while," he recalled, "I was afraid to bend over. The mere sight of my undefended rear end must have had the same appeal as a beefsteak." Dogs were the bane of his existence. "I always thought they had some secret society among the mongrels, with a prize to the one who took the biggest chunk of flesh out of me," he theorized. But he also had a simpler explanation: "A dog knew a tramp when he sniffed one."

With the arrival of autumn, the demand for ice dwindled, and he sought other employment. He soon found a job as a newsboy. When he made a sale, he performed with a flourish and the grand manner, prompting a buyer to remark, "It was as if he were handing me the crown jewels."

So far as he was concerned, no paper contained dull reading. He made each edition seem really worth buying, and his headline hyperbole caused prospective purchasers to believe either that the world was coming to an end or that the nation was about to plunge into war. He was adroit at conceiving crazy names for fictitious news items, such as: *Amos Stump Discovered Living in Eagle's Nest.*

Should a buyer ever complain that he could find no such story, Woody apologized profusely. "My dear sir, you were the victim of a printer's error. Due to a mechanical imperfection, three papers out of a run of thousands failed to carry the item." The explanation was generally satisfactory, and the complainer began to think he had won some form of lottery by being one of the lucky three.

More and more he began to concentrate on his juggling. Balls, cigar boxes, and hats became his specialty. His supply of hats was unlimited, the source being an Elks' social where Woody and a chum entered the cloakroom through a window and left the same way with armfuls of men's hats. Keeping an oversized one for himself, Woody said, "If the cops are after me, it covers my entire face."

He began to land jobs, first with carnivals, then finally working up a couple of rungs on the entertainment ladder to Fortescue's Pier in Atlantic City where he was billed as "W.C. Fields, Tramp Juggler." Later he began to introduce a wheezy-twanged dialogue to accompany the various objects he threw into the air.

Trying to collect a paycheck from Fortescue's Pier became an impossibility, so he joined a road show where he juggled and understudied several dramatic roles—one of them that of an elderly woman—until the company went bankrupt. From then on it was one poorly paying job after another.

His mind was never idle, for in it he was filing original comedy bits he hoped to do some day.

He joined another road show and toured for a man named Fred Irwin. He had no contract—a custom of those days which ordinarily favored the manager. But not so in the case of the Tramp Juggler. Woody was a past master at badgering for a raise. The most effective method was to wave a handful of favorable press clippings in the manager's face.

At the age of nineteen Woody broke into vaudeville, eventually receiving a salary of $125 per week. Vacillating between Keith's and the Orpheum circuits, he added more dialogue and a trick pool table to his act. This was taking a chance, because pool was not exactly a game of high social standing. But his clever manipulation with a cue that was not only bumpy and knotty, but crooked as well, convulsed audiences.

For a number of years he toured England to play Command Performances for King Edward VII at Buckingham Palace, crossed to the Continent for an extensive European tour, and in following years his travels included Australia, South Africa and the Orient. It was in Cape Town that he first met Will Rogers, with whom he would later co-star in the *Ziegfeld Follies*.

His musical show career started in 1915 with *Watch Your Step*, an Irving Berlin musical. He watched his step—and found it led to nowhere. After a single month he bombed out. A note had been left in his dressing room by Gene Buck, Ziegfeld's righthand man: "See you in New York if anything goes wrong."

Woody turned up in his office two days later, his blond hair parted down the middle, wearing a long fake black mustache, explaining, "I'm disguised in case any of the *Watch Your Step* audience should spot me."

Buck put him in the *Follies*.

From 1915 through 1921 he starred in the *Follies* and the press hailed him as a "distinguished comedian." He also appeared in *George White's Scandals*, other musicals, and in some legitimate plays, including *Poppy*.

Then it was on to Hollywood after an outstanding record of stage successes, with a feeble sprinkling of motion pictures made on Long Island.

Four

To paraphrase Woody, sometimes good comes out of an earthquake: His incapacity due to his broken coccyx caused a cessation of hostilities in the kitchen and servants' quarters. An air of peace—transient though it might be—descended upon the household, but I suppose you might more accurately describe it as an armed truce.

Keeping his domestics in a turmoil—it mattered little if they were cooks, butlers or chauffeurs—was part of his master plan of life.

By fiendishly planting false rumors, he'd pit one domestic against the other, moving them about like pieces on a chessboard. He was a director of organized confusion, misunderstanding, bedlam, distrust, and waging a continual battle against happiness, he always emerged the victor. But his troops were expendable. After a court-martial or a voluntary turning in of uniform, Woody could always call an employment agency for replacements who were unaware they were walking into a lion's den.

I think that Della, his diminutive sepia-colored cook, was actually the only servant that he admired over the years. But even Della was not spared of his plottings. There was a period of nearly three months when she barely spoke to me, and then only when absolutely necessary. After weeks of trying futilely to corner her conversationally, wanting desperately to get to the bottom of her silent treatment, I managed to pry open her lips.

"Mr. Fields says you don't like my cooking," she confessed.

"That's not true."

"He says you think I use too many spices." She seemed ready to cry. I threw my arms around her making it clear that *nothing* could be too spicy for a girl who was part Mexican, and told her of the time I had eaten an entire jar of hot Mexican chili peppers. Much to Mr. Fields' anger, they had brought out blisters on my backside! I explained that Mr. Fields wasn't *really* a liar, but that he enjoyed spreading false rumors and watching the reactions they caused; and that he got a kick from moving people about like puppets, from manipulating their lives and stirring up tempests. This, I told Della, was what made him happiest.

As another example, I recall a butler named John whom Woody swore was trying to poison him. "I can see him now," he said, lowering his head and covering his eyes with his hands to emulate a seer peering into the future. "Leaning over my grave and spitting on it."

"Well then, fire him," I suggested.

"Perish the thought," he said indignantly. "Why, that would eliminate one of my problems."

As it turned out, John died while in Woody's employ. Woody summed up his remorse by stating, "He must have been awful hungry to sample some of the poisoned food he intended serving me," but then went ahead and took care of the funeral expenses and sent a check for $500 to the deceased servant's widow.

While his coccyx was mending, I nursed him back to health. I had to make sure not to tuck his covers in at the foot of his bed, since his feet had to stick out during the night and get fresh air, or he couldn't sleep. He claimed this was a throwback to his youth, a habit developed when the cold, wintry breezes blew through the holes in his shoe soles. He added that he always had had to walk around carefully to avoid stepping on lighted matches.

He read constantly during his convalescence—some Mark Twain, but mostly Dickens. Woody was an avid Dickens buff, and once gave me a copy of *David Copperfield* which he had autographed himself: "To Carlotta, with love for her kindness when I needed it most." He particularly loved and always chuckled over the names of nearly all of the sixteen-hundred characters, both major and minor, used by the English writer, such as Minnie Meagles, Mr. Pip, Bertha Plummer, Miss Robina Buffle, Miss Sophronia Akershem, Clarence Barnacle, Silas Jones Jorgan, La Fayette Kettle, Mortimer Lightwood, Miss Henrietta Nupkins, Mrs. Mary Peerybingle, Miss Amelia Crumpton, Thomas Bladerstone, the Cheeryble Brothers, Uriah Heep, Mark Tapley, Horatio Fizkin, The Honorable Samuel Slumkey, Miss Isabella Wardle, Lady Snuphanuph, Augustus Snodgrass, Mrs. Creakle, Miss Murdstone, Mr. Omer, Mr. Barkis, Mr. Pidge, Miss Rosa Dartle, Miss Mowcher, and Mrs. Gummidge.

There's no doubt in my mind that the fictitious names Woody used during his movie making were inspired by Dickens characters—names like Professor Eustace McGargle, Elmer Prettywillie, Samuel Bisbee, Elmer Finch, Gabby Gilfoil, Professor Quail, Augustus Winterbottom, Harold Bissonette, Ambrose Wolfinger, T. Frothingwell Bellows, Larson E. Whipsnade, Cuthbert Twillie, Egbert Sousé, Woolchester Cowperthwaite.

Notice the resemblance?

By his bedside were *A Christmas Carol, Great Expectations, David Copperfield, Nicholas Nickleby, The Old Curiosity Shop, Oliver Twist, Martin Chuzzlewit, The Pickwick Papers,* and *Our Mutual Friend.*

I asked if he had any favorite Dickens characters.

Without hesitation, he answered, "Fagin, Scrooge and Micawber."

"Why those three?" I wanted to know.

"Fagin was an unkempt old man, a thief who taught children to steal—which, of course, started a youngster off in a profitable business. Fagin was important. He was unforgettable, and his name eventually reached Webster's dictionary.

"As for Micawber, he was a rapscallion, a scallywag, the archetype of the joyously improvident opportunist." Then Woody's face lit up. "But oh, that Ebenezer Scrooge! He was a character after my own heart. Let me read you a description of him."

He leafed through *A Christmas Carol* to find what he was seeking. " '*Oh! but he was a tight-fisted hand at the grindstone, Scrooge!—a squeezing, wrenching, grasping, clutching, covetous old sinner. Hard and sharp as flint, from which no steel had ever struck out generous fire; secret and self-contained and solitary as an oyster. The cold within him froze his old features, nipped his pointed nose, shrivelled his cheek, stiffened his gait, made his eyes red, his thin lips blue, and spoke out shrewdly in his grating voice. A frosty rime was on his head, and on his eyebrows and his wiry chin. He carried his own low temperature always about with him; he iced his office in the dogdays and didn't thaw it one degree at Christmas.*' "

I gasped, "You mean that you admire this—this . . ."

"Please," he interrupted, "do not, I warn you, cast aspersions on my personal idol. I love the man. I think he should replace George Washington and Abraham Lincoln in our schoolbooks—only he fell from my good graces at the end of the tale."

"How?" I questioned.

"He reformed, that's what the blithering idiot did," Woody roared. "He became benevolent." He raised his voice and began to shout, "That was Dickens' only mistake! He allowed Scrooge to get out of character!"

Woody, I learned, had no sentiment about Christmas, a day

on which he generally gave me a hundred dollars. Probing his dislike of the holiday, he said it stemmed from childhood days. He had been saving up enough money to buy his mother a present, hiding the coins and bills inside a milk bottle in the basement, and then, "A bastard I knew stole it," he complained.

"A former friend?" I asked.

"You might call him that," he said. "He was my father."

To him, the celebrated English writer was a master of dialogue. He devoured the Victorian stilted phrases, and would mark passages from various books that appealed to him, like the following from *David Copperfield*:

"Hey! What did he die of?" asked my aunt.

"Well, ma'am, he died of drink," said Mrs. Crupp, in confidence. "And smoke."

"Smoke? You don't mean chimneys?" said my aunt.

"No, ma'am," returned Mrs. Crupp. "Cigars and pipes."

"That's not catching, at any rate," remarked my aunt turning to me.

"No, indeed," said I.

Woody also loved the lines uttered by Mrs. Micawber before her husband is thrown into a debtors' prison: *"I never thought, before I was married, when I lived with Papa and Mamma, that I should ever find it necessary to take a lodger* (the boy, David Copperfield). *But Mr. Micawber being in difficulties, all considerations of private feeling must give way. If Mr. Micawber's creditors* will not *give him time, they must take the consequences. Blood cannot be obtained from a stone, neither can anything on account be obtained at present from Mr. Micawber."*

Micawber's own dialogue intrigued him, such as the paragraph where there was a chance meeting with David Copperfield:

"My dear Copperfield, this is indeed a meeting which is calculated to impress the mind with a sense of the instability of all humans—in short, it is a most extraordinary meeting.

Walking along the street, reflecting upon the probability of something turning up (of which I am at present rather sanguine), I find a young but valued friend turn up. Copperfield, how do you do?"

He was equally fond of the heartrending letter Micawber penned to young Copperfield:

My dear young friend,

The die is cast—all is over. Hiding the ravages of care with a sickly mask of mirth, I have not informed you . . . that there is no hope of the remittance! Under these circumstances, alike . . . humiliating to relate, I have discharged the pecuniary liability contracted at this establishment, by giving a note of hand, made payable fourteen days after date. . . . When it becomes due, it will not be taken up. The result is destruction. The bolt is impending, and the tree must fall.

Let the wretched man who now addresses you, my dear Copperfield, be a beacon to you through life. He writes with that intention. . . . If he could think himself of so much use, one gleam of day might . . . penetrate into the cheerless dungeon of his remaining existence—though his longevity is, at present (to say the least of it), extremely problematical.

This is the last communication, my dear Copperfield, you will ever receive

From the Beggared Outcast, Wilkins Micawber

Dickens, Woody said, was easy to read and easy to remember —and the latter was what he wanted the public to do after viewing his films. "I like my films to influence the audience," he said. "Even if it means tripping their aged grandparents with a cane when they get home."

He labeled Dickens "the bravest man who ever lived. He fathered ten children before they became tax deductions." "Dickens," he said seriously, "was the most popular writer the world has ever known. He was not appreciated in his day, nor for many years following his death. His plots were called unwieldy and his characters unreal. Now, upon examination, critics have reversed their earlier opinions. The man must have been good if Dostoevski was his pupil. What Dickens had was imagination—it was unsurpassed. And his character delineations were superb. They simply walked off the pages into your life, to live on with you until the end of your days."

Dead though he might be, I was almost jealous of Charles Dickens.

Woody was convinced that many people knew of Dickens but never got around to reading him. "There's a special shelf devoted to him in nearly every library," he said. "Few men go near it because far too few men go into a library. Men generally are afraid of libraries. They feel inferior in one. They usually have to ask a female librarian how to find anything."

I need hardly mention his delight when M-G-M offered him the part of Micawber in the film version of *David Copperfield*, which was released in 1935. "The world will now know of the art of Dickens," he vowed.

But the cast—which included Lionel Barrymore, Maureen O'Sullivan, Madge Evans, Edna May Oliver, Lewis Stone, Freddie Bartholomew, Roland Young, Basil Rathbone, and Elsa Lanchester—was dismayed upon learning that Woody was to play one of the roles. "Whoever heard of a pool table and juggling act in anything of Dickens'?" came the wail.

David O. Selznick, the producer, and director George Cukor, harbored no fears that the comedian would try to make *David Copperfield* a showcase for himself and dredge up some of his favorite props. At the conclusion of the shooting, Mr. Cukor stated: "This was the only movie part that Fields ever played that he didn't re-create. He dreamed up nothing. For the first time in his career he followed the script, probably because of his admiration for Dickens. The part of Micawber was perfect for him. He was born to play it. Fields and Micawber were interchangeable. His part was short but important.

"It looked for a while that Charles Laughton was going to get the part. But it wasn't quite right for him. When asked to do it, Fields jumped at the chance. I found him most amenable, most cooperative in every way. I saw no indication of the legend built up about him. The man was helpful, on his good behavior, very dignified. So many stories concerning Fields had been poured, unasked for, into my ears that I was ready for some display of outrageous conduct. Even his trademark—a hatred for children—was not in evidence. Freddie Bartholomew was eleven years old at the time the film was made, and Fields treated him royally. To a stranger he might have seemed to be Fields' own son."

What Mr. Cukor said is true. I was with Woody during almost every minute of the making of this picture. His disposition was sunny from beginning to end, and he welcomed anyone in the cast to his dressing room for coffee or drinking breaks. The only improvising he did was in a shaving scene of Micawber's. Wielding a long straight-edged razor like a saber, he made passes at his jugular vein that convulsed the cast. Someone cut out the scene but Woody didn't seem to mind. ". . . was probably too young to have shaved and didn't realize the perils," he excused. I thought it should have been left in. If Dickens wrote it and Woody elaborated on it, who could dispute this powerful collaboration?

Certainly he was on his best behavior during the *David Copperfield* filming.

Rebel that he was, Woody usually refused to obey any suggestion even if it were for his own good. If anyone merely suggested, "Bill, you must do this or that, or see some screen offering," he'd display a mulish stubbornness and do just the opposite. He was his own man, no doubt about it, and no one was going to change his habits, which he once described as "lousy, but perfect for me."

In a moment of pique I had once decided to instigate a few reforms through a sort of low-key campaign. But during his recuperation period I got to know him better, and right then and there I swore that so long as I lived under the same roof with him, I'd go along with his raffish ways; I'd never attempt to make him over or act as a brake on his activities, be what they may. Only when they were harmful—like excessive drinking—would I try to temper a habit.

Woody antedated today's protestors by many years. He was a one-man forerunner of what was to be, truculently opposing all authority. Single-handedly he wanted to fight the entire social system.

Years later, Mr. Cukor said of Fields, "Whatever he did that caused people to call him a rapscallion, he left the public something that they adored. Especially young people. He seems to be their banner waver. They queue up for blocks to hand over three dollars to see two of his one-hour pictures."

Woody was constantly at war against what the younger generation now terms "the Establishment." This attitude of his is probably the reason for the growing W.C. Fields cult. I've often thought that if he were alive today and still kicking up his usual storm of rebellion, dissenting student marchers would paint his bulbous nose on their signs as a red, steadily glowing symbol of defiance, a mutinous banner to wave in the square face of convention.

He did what he wanted to do, regardless of the consequences. If he wanted to pick a flower on someone's private property, he plucked. He was fined several times for this act.

He was the antithesis (one of his favorite words) of his friend, Will Rogers. The cowboy humorist is credited with saying "I never met a man I didn't like." Fields was suspicious of all but a handful of people he met. He figured most of them wanted something from him. Of him, Will Rogers said, "Thank God he's a comic. Had he been a statesman he'd have plunged the world into total war."

His hardest and longest fight was against regimentation. Had he been inducted into the army, he might have tried the manual-of-arms drill with his famous crooked pool cue. This I can safely say: Any branch of the service would have cashiered him within two weeks for disobeying orders. And if he had been handed a dishonorable discharge, he would have had the certificate laminated and proudly hung in his den.

In many private wars created by his own volition, he won more verbal battles than he lost. Never did he plummet to total defeat because, somehow, he always managed to get in the last word—if the angry, wheezing sounds coming from his throat could be classified as words.

A sacred cow to him was only a hunk of meat to be barbecued. Among his pet hates in life were doctors, lawyers, children, dogs, henpecking, literary and pedantic women, script writers, studio property men, churchgoers, bluenoses, bankers, and the Internal Revenue Service.

The Bureau of Internal Revenue, as it was called in those days, stirred his particular anger: He felt sure that those representatives of our government devoted a full eight hours daily, with no lunch breaks, to catching him in error. I'll always remember the evening when an attorney came over to help him with his income tax. Hearing some angry cries, I went into his office either to stop or at least to referee the fight I heard in progress.

When I entered the room I saw an irate Woody standing and shouting at a small, bespectacled man. "A multitude of curses upon you, sir! You want to know my definition of a lawyer?" I'm sure the attorney couldn't care less, but Woody growled, "There are seven natural openings in the head and body. A lawyer is the only human being with eight. The extra one is a slot to store money in, should his bank be unable to hold all of it."

His face livid, the attorney angrily jammed some papers into his briefcase, rose, and said, "I'll find my own way out, Mr. Fields."

"After six years of college you should be able to," Woody shouted after him.

I eased Woody into a chair and rubbed his neck—which often had a calming effect—and asked what the trouble was.

"I figure I drink an average of forty-two ounces of liquor daily," he recounted, "which totals 14,700 ounces yearly. At fifty cents per ounce at a bar, which is the popular price, the total tab comes to $7,350."

"But you don't drink at public bars," I interrupted.

"Well, that's for the government to find out. They've got spies infiltrating into everything. At any rate, $7,350 is a pretty nice chunk of deduction."

"But, Woody, how can you deduct alcohol?"

"Because I use it purely for medicinal purposes," he answered straight-faced.

"Is that the reason you had a fight with your attorney?"

"Of course. Why else? The stupid sonofabitch claimed it wasn't deductible. Lawyers! Bah! Humbug! The income tax was devised to give lawyers and certified public accountants business. Few persons can make head, tail, or middle out of it. Einstein admitted he couldn't. Why, we once had a president who, surrounded by all his high-priced advisors, paid a thousand dollars too much on his tax return. So how could the average taxpayer, like Xavier P. Zilt or W.C. Fields, be expected to do it correctly? It hardly pays to be in an upper bracket. Then a man worries whether he's going to jail or if he's being cheated by the government."

While he was bedridden, his faithful followers kept trooping in to visit him. They brought crazy gag presents. "If you really want to cheer me up," Woody told Barrymore, "Bring money. And never mind the gift wrapping. A large rubber band will do nicely."

One day an interviewer from a national magazine telephoned for an appointment, and after consulting his schedule, Woody asked me to set it up for a certain time. It was quite unusual for him to regard writers and journalists in a kindly light, and he always scoffed at the custom many stars adopted of hiring a personal publicist. His own excuse was, "Some prison warden might recognize my picture and identify me as Number 74896207235648 who once went over the wall." As a result there was a dearth of articles on him in magazines and newspapers.

The interviewer who came out to the house was young and excited, titillated by the prospect of an interview with the great W.C. Fields. He was so nervous that as he unscrewed the top of his fountain pen it rolled under a couch, and when he got down on his hands and knees to retrieve it, he bumped his head.

Woody shifted the toothpick in his mouth—something he was rarely without—and explained, "Have to carry one of these in case they forget to stick one in the martini olive. Good to have a spare around, you know."

Among the first questions he was asked was, "What is your conception of heaven?"

Woody eyed him suspiciously. "You some kind of a preacher, son?"

The young man stoutly denied the accusation.

"I'll tell you my conception of heaven, young man," Woody began.

The interviewer leaned forward eagerly, thinking this would be a rich plum, a real scoop: the religious beliefs of W.C. Fields. Did he worship God or mammon? Was he an atheist? Agnostic?

"It's quite simple. I'd take a doctor and a lawyer—pick any two at random from the telephone directory—and strap each into a chair facing the other. First the lawyer gives the doctor legal advice, and when the doctor asks, 'How much do I owe you?' the lawyer is gagged before he can answer. The same is repeated with the doctor.

"In this way neither collects a cent, which is just about what they're collectively worth, and to be a witness to this would be heaven to me."

The interviewer tried again. "Do you have a formula that might be applied to a person wishing to get rich?"

"Yes, when the little beggar is only ten years old, have him castrated and his taste buds destroyed. He'll grow up never needing a woman, a steak or a cigarette. Think of the money saved," Woody replied. Foolishness such as this answer was the order of the day, as hyperbolical nonsense rolled off his well-oiled tongue. Periodically he would pause and ask the interviewer seriously, "Didn't I meet you in Sing Sing many years ago?"

The young man took out a handkerchief and wiped perspiration from his forehead, although the room temperature was quite comfortable. "What are your views on marriage, Mr. Fields?"

"Marriage?" Woody repeated as if he had never heard the word. "Ah yes, marriage. I believe in tying the marriage knot, as long as it's around the woman's neck." He then proceeded to deliver the following series of epigrams:

"Marriage is a two-way proposition, but never let the woman know she is one of the ways.

"In marriage a man must give up many of his old and pleasant habits, even if it means giving up the woman he married.

"Always have a woman sign a prenuptial agreement that if she leaves your bed and board, she takes off with as little cash as possible.

"Marry an outdoors woman. Then if you throw her out into the yard for the night, she can still survive.

"Marriage is better than leprosy because it's easier to get rid of.

"Never trust your wife behind your back, even if she claims she only wants to wash or scratch it.

"An ideal start for matrimony would be to have a drunken rabbi perform a Catholic ceremony in an Episcopalian church. Then it could be declared illegal in the courts."

(The next day I opened my trusty notebook, deciphered the scribblings, and asked Woody if he recalled his observations on marriage. He not only remembered, but his retentive mind was able to repeat his views sentence by sentence.)

When his interviewer seemed stumped and undecided as to what question to pose next, Woody advised, "Why don't you commit some minor crime, son? And when you get out of jail, come see me and you'll be able to understand me better."

Undaunted, the interrogator continued: "What was the most unpleasant experience you ever had, Mr. Fields?"

Woody hesitated five or six seconds, then snapped his fingers. "That's easy to remember. The time a hot, sticky baby jumped onto my lap and called me 'Daddy!'"

"What did you do, Mr. Fields?"

"What did I do, son? Why, I did the only thing I could do —the only course any redblooded man could pursue to keep his honesty and integrity and standing in the community. I simply opened my legs and catapulted him on his head. Never forget the sound—brings back a flood of wonderful memories. Sounded like a ripe melon squashed by a sledgehammer."

For the first time the interviewer dropped his serious mien, and playing along, asked, "What happened to the child?"

"Grew up to become one of the most important men in Hollywood. Now the brains of a giant studio," Woody rasped.

"Did you ever wish to be in any line of work besides acting?"

"Yes," Woody answered readily, "safecracking. Too much noise on the eardrums, though. I have sensitive eardrums."

The young man left the house with his head spinning, muttering something unintelligible that seemed to translate to, "Let me out of here." Formerly he'd achieved a few bylines, but I didn't hear of him after his visit with us—that is, in the literary field. I asked Woody about him and he said, "There's a rumor he took up plumbing."

The young man was not alone in his failure. The majority of interviewers who tried to mine the rich mother lode of Fieldsian humor—wide veins of pure, solid comedy—came up with empty typewriters. Only Alva Johnson succeeded fairly well in a 1938 *Saturday Evening Post* article.

* * * * * * * * * *

Almost every celebrity has at least a few skeletons hidden in the family closet. But for Woody's closet there were no locks or keys. He'd trot everything out for inspection. He discussed his thefts and imprisonments unashamedly. Whether they were fact or fiction, no one was sure. At each opportunity—and he'd create many of them—he downgraded himself, freely blackening his own character, and few of his answers were fit to print. Here are some examples:

Question: "What is your chief fear, Mr. Fields?"
"A venereal disease."

Question: "Have you ever been exposed to a great risk?"
"Yes. Sitting on a toilet seat after Greg La Cava just got off."

Question: "Do retakes on the set bother you?"
"Well . . . let me ponder that question. Yes, yes, they do. Only one in my life didn't. Gave me complete satisfaction. Even ecstasy. I was working with Baby LeRoy, and the kid dipped my watch in molasses. I kicked him about ten feet. The director thought the boot was too prodigious and that wonderful, thoughtful man called for a retake. Now, that's the kind of a retake I like. Sir, I'll say it once and I'll say it again and again—there's not a man in America who at one time or another hasn't had a secret desire to boot a child squarely in the ass."

Five

BESIDES attempting to get him to cut down on liquor, I tried to temper his profane outbursts. I was a Catholic then and a fairly religious one, and every time he took the Lord's name in vain I'd raise my eyes toward the heavens and plead, "Forgive him, oh Lord, for he knows not what he's saying."

"Goddam it," he'd snap back, "I do so."

Woody had no religion, claiming that his only appearance in a church was in some little Pennsylvania town when he broke a stained glass window in order to sleep warmly in one of the pews.

"I think of the church often," he said. "Not because religion was closing in on me, but because for a long time my ass was sore from that hard, unupholstered pew."

He frequently challenged God to strike him down or to give him more pain than he already had. When there was no response, he would turn to me gloatingly and say, "See, Chinaman? Nothing happened!"

Then among his book collection I found a dog-eared Gideon Bible. "You old fraud," I accused, "you're the softest hardboiled egg I ever knew." I held up the book for him to see. "It shows considerable use."

"Termites," he said.

"Better think up a better one than that," I told him.

"I've never opened it," he claimed. "I stole it in Lansing, Michigan. The man who had the room before me kept reading it from cover to cover. He was trying to save his soul from the fires of purgatory."

"Do you expect me to believe that?"

"Well, now, Chinaman," he said, "I admit I scanned it once, searching for some movie plots."

"Find any?"

"Only a pack of wild lies."

"Care to tell me about them?" I wandered over to a tape recorder I had given him as a present. It was an early, experimental, wire model, not yet manufactured on a large commercial scale. It had cost me $950, the result of months of saving. He was crazy over it. He didn't see me turn it on and plug it in.

He lit a long cigar and began an even longer dissertation—I guess you might call it a debunking:

The Gospel According to Woody "To me, these Biblical stories are just so many fish stories, and I'm not specifically referring to Jonah and the whale. I need indisputable proof of anything I'm asked to believe. Someone has to come up with the whys and the wherefores. For example, in the beginning Adam and Eve were very happy and contented, as well they should be with no work, no income tax, no lawyers, no doctors, no children, no dogs, surrounded by food-bearing trees and edible plants. They were vegetarians, but not by choice.

"In the middle of this paradise stood the forbidden tree.

"But up slithered a serpent to tempt Eve, encouraging her to sample the fruit and practically guaranteeing 'You shall not die.' It is little wonder, then, that if a serpent could tempt Eve with a piece of fruit, such tangibles as diamonds could easily sway members of her sex in the thousands of years that followed.

"Eve gave Adam some of the fruit. It was delicious, and the young couple probably gorged themselves. God, of course, discovering their transgression, banished them from the garden forever.

"As a matter of fact, the serpent got the worst of the deal. He was despised by all living creatures—except herpetologists—and relegated to crawl upon the earth. This inferred that if the serpent had not fallen from the Lord's good graces, we would be conversant with all snakes today, from rattlers to garter snakes, thus enabling them to put forth strong talking points against extermination.

"It's all in the Bible.

"Take Noah's Ark. Noah and his family walked and talked with God—or so they claimed. They were His favorites. But not so the other people, who were wicked and continually quarreling with one another. The Lord spoke to Noah and said 'I shall bring a flood of waters upon the earth, to destroy all living things from under heaven, and everything that is on the earth shall die,' or words to that effect. Just why the beasts, the creeping things and the birds were to be punished for the misdeeds of humans remains unexplained.

"He advised Noah to be ensconced in the ark with his entire family before the rains came and guaranteed him safety. With him should be two of every living thing—the birds and beasts and everything that crept—except a few doctors I know—and he was to take food for all who were aboard.

"One point I'd like clarified is, where did Noah and sons get tools enough for this monumental task? Think of all the food necessary and the storage space required. Not all the animals were herbiverous. How was meat kept fresh before the days of refrigeration? Why, a crew of dozens would have been essential to shovel away the offal and dump it overboard. Another Leviathan with a specially trained and full crew would have been necessary. And the ship would have taken years to construct and assemble and launch. Jonah didn't even have a pilot's license. And where did he learn navigation?

"Both God and Noah appeared to have forgotten the anchor —certainly a necessity on any ship.

"Readers of the Old Testament are aware it rained for forty days and forty nights. Noah must have been a brilliant student of weather conditions. His instruments for foretelling barometric changes were a raven and a dove. They flew from an open window—Noah evidently never heard of a porthole—to use their sharp eyes to see if the waters were receding.

"Because Captain Noah used the term 'window' any seaman would have classified him as a landlubber. While Noah may not have understood navigation, he certainly understood bird life, for the released dove returned after a few days, which meant there had been no place for a dry landing.

"No mention of the raven was made. To this day it is missing. Actually, the raven would have been a more reliable bird than the dove, for if the raven of Edgar Allen Poe could quoth 'Nevermore,' Noah's bird might have been able to chirp 'Land ho!'

"Noah rested the dove and then sent the bird forth again in seven days. This time the dove returned with an olive leaf in her mouth. There was no way of ascertaining whether the olives from the tree found by the dove were colossal, mammoth, large, giant, pitted or unpitted.

"And God spoke to Noah again and urged him—after the ark rested on Mt. Ararat and the lands dried up—to depart from the ark with his sons and their wives and the rest of the passengers which were the beasts, the creeping things, and the birds.

"Last to leave were the tortoises and the insects, and as far as I'm concerned they could have left the dratted mosquitoes aboard.

"God blessed Noah and his sons and said unto them: 'Be fruitful and replenish the earth.'

"Everyone who had been aboard started propagating, and the first population explosion was recorded.

"Now, Chinaman, if you want to believe this nonsense, that is your privilege. Yet perhaps there *is* a lesson to be learned: What the world needs today is another flood of hemispheric proportions.

"The flight of the Jews from Egypt, where six hundred thousand of them were held in slavery, is another doubtful story. Moses said to Pharaoh, 'Set my people free.' When Pharoah refused, Moses told him, 'If you don't let my people go, the Lord will send plagues and pestilence to Egypt.' Pharaoh laughed at this threat, but not for long. Soon the following chain of events, much to the displeasure of the Egyptians, occurred:

A. A swarm of flies covered the people, the cattle, the land.
B. Frogs were overrunning the country.
C. Some unknown pest killed all the Egyptians' cattle, sparing the cows of the Israelites.
D. All rivers and water in Egypt turned to blood.
E. Terrible hail and lightning and thunder such as was never before known and which broke down every tree in the field and destroyed every herb, came from the skies.

"This seemed to be more than Pharoah and his people could bear. He called Moses and Aaron, and promised that if Moses got the Lord to relent and halt the devastating storm, he would let the Israelites go.

"Moses then lifted his hand to the Lord, and weather conditions immediately changed.

"That wasn't the only change. Pharaoh again changed his

mind. Angered by the trickery, the Lord dispatched locusts to swarm over Egypt.

"Again Pharaoh made a false promise, and again the Lord retaliated—this time by having darkness overspread Egypt, except in the houses of the Israelites where the lights were brighter than ever. This didn't bother Pharaoh too much, as he was fond of dancing girls and they looked twice as attractive in the dark.

"So God thought of something drastic that would bring the Egyptian ruler to his knees. 'All firstborn'—Pharaoh's own, those of the people and the beasts—'will die,' He decreed. But the children of Israel would be unharmed.

"The Lord carried out His threat. This was the straw that broke the back of Pharaoh's camel. Now he kept his word and freed the Israelites with their flocks and their herds. They departed, but Pharaoh, who seemed to change his mind more often than a woman does her drapes, did so again, and sent his soldiers in speedy pursuit, with the hope of again making slaves of the Israelites.

"The Children of Moses fled to the waters of the Red Sea, where they no longer retreated. The sea was to their backs. Their position appeared untenable.

"Suddenly part of the sea turned into dry land, the Children of Israel walked across to the other shore. The Egyptian soldiers tried to emulate this feat with all their chariots and horses, but in the middle of the sea the waters rose and rushed over them. None escaped a watery grave.

"Is this fiction or factual? You decide, Chinaman.

"I think the Jews are a wonderfully clever people who from season to season might offer prayers that the sun shine over Miami Beach in the winter so they can return north with fine suntans. But to be able, as Joshua did on request, to keep Old Sol suspended in the sky and eliminate night falling, is something I can't buy.

"An additional absurdity is the story of Jonah and the whale. To me this tall tale is a lot of blubber. Or a lot of whale oil. Take your choice.

"Should it be true, then Jonah—one of the minor prophets —did such a whale of a job by managing to live in a sea monster's belly for three days before being regurgitated upon the land, that he deserved promotion in the ranks of the prophets. Maybe that's what he was really bucking for.

"To believe Daniel in the lion's den—Never.

"Daniel, it seemed, was a babe in the woods where politics were concerned. He was on good terms with a number of people who he thought were his friends, but who turned out to be asps in the grass. Actually, he could afford a few enemies, considering that his best and most loyal friend was the king.

"Daniel had two weaknesses in the eyes of his subordinates: He was faithful and honest, which many will agree are rather bad and unusual traits. There must be a way to get to him, they thought, and after sitting up many nights and burning many candles, a sneaky plan evolved.

"A delegation went to the king and asked him to sign a decree that if anyone should ask a favor of God or man, except the king, he should be thrown into the den of lions.

"The naïve king signed the decree. Then one day the schemers found Daniel praying to his God. They reported this act to the king. According to law, the decree could not be altered and Daniel was scheduled for the lions.

"You see, Daniel had been one of the Children of Israel captured in Judah, and he was guilty of praying to his own Lord three times daily.

"Against his will the king sentenced Daniel to the lions, but comforted him with the words, 'Daniel, thy God, whom thou servest continually, will save thee'—and today would have added, 'from becoming a lionburger.'

"In those days the lions were toothy, hungry animals, unlike the circus ones of today who jump upon stools and pay homage to their masters—the men with the bullwhips. As pictures of Daniel showed him as not exactly skinny, the animals were due to feast on a choice cut.

"The king, slightly worried over the possible fate of his friend, ordered all music stopped in the palace and passed a sleepless night of fasting. Very early the next morning he went to see Daniel, or whatever remained of him.

"He praised, 'Oh Daniel, servant of the living God, thank God, your God saved you,' or something of that sort.

"Daniel put the king's fears to rest as he replied, 'Oh king, live forever. My God sent an angel that shut the lions' mouths, for I have done no harm to thee, nor to anyone, oh king.'

"The king was happy and ordered Daniel to be brought up from the lions' den. It was found he had suffered no wounds. Then—possibly because the cost of feeding the lions was mounting—the king commanded that the accusers of Daniel be cast into the den. No angels came to the rescue. Thus were the lions not deprived of fresh meat.

"Am I so gullible that I'd actually believe that a cherubic little fellow known as an angel and carrying a harp in one hand, visited a den full of hungry lions, to go around closing their mouths, one by one?

* * * * * * * * * *

"Samson the Strong was a many-muscled young man whose career was studded with superhuman feats of strength.

"The Philistines needed to discover his weakness—if any—and who was better suited for the task than a temptress named Delilah? The tantalizing movements of her supple body might in themselves have been sufficient to pry forth the secret of Samson's strength, but she was a smart girl who decided to use the one weapon guaranteed to make a man tell all: tears. Her open tear ducts opened Samson's lips, and he revealed that his strength was in his long hair, and if it were sheared he would be as weak as the average man.

"While Samson slept, Delilah got a man to shave his head.

Now robbed of his extraordinary muscles, the Philadelphians—I mean the Philistines—put out his eyes and threw him into prison. But they forgot one thing: Hair on a young man not suffering from baldness will grow. This is exactly what happened.

"One day, three thousand Philistines gathered in a temple to make sacrifices to one of the idols they worshipped. They sent for Samson to mock and make sport of the helpless blind man. A boy led him to the throng, most of whom were gathered under the flat temple roof. Samson asked the boy to place his hands on the pillars of the building.

"He prayed to the Lord for strength, pressed against the pillars of the building, and the roof caved in. All were killed. Among them Samson.

"Here again is a tall tale to devour. I've watched some of the strongest men in the world—the weight lifters—pressing and jerking four hundred pound weights, but none of them, I'm sure, could even dent the pillar of a great building.

"Having been a spectator at the famous Dempsey-Firpo fight and seen with my own eyes a man called a giant killer, I might be able to go along with the feat of David who, the Bible tells us, slew Goliath with the jawbone of an ass—if I didn't read how big this giant was supposed to be. Somehow I have the feeling that the giant would have knocked David on *his* ass.

"In the Bible, Peter, a man who worked dozens of miracles for other folks but none for himself, was cast into prison where he was guarded day and night by soldiers. Both his right and left arms were chained to the wrists of soldiers. Even Harry Houdini might have found it tough to escape from this one.

"But not if he were sponsored by a little angel who was waiting in the wings. A bright light shone in Peter's cell the moment he was awakened by something striking him on the side. Looking up from his straw bed, he saw a gorgeous angel standing over him. He first thought it was Mae West, until he realized he was slightly before her time.

" 'Rise up quickly,' the angel commanded. The chains dropped off and Peter, accompanied by the guardian angel, walked out of the prison to the great iron gate of the city which opened wide for them.

"In all these Biblical stories the angels fly around more than the planes at a busy airport terminal. They must have been pretty smart pilots for I never heard of a single collision. Why, they never even get their wings snarled. A man like me needs proof, and no one has come forward with proof that there are or were angels. I've seen plenty of pictures of them, though— always white angels. Where were the black ones? Maybe a deserving dead Negro became a white angel. If so, this was really Heaven beyond his greatest expectation.

"Angels hardly ever seemed too energetic. All they ever did was sit on a soft cloud and strum away on a harp. I thought that would be kind of a monotonous life for a man who frequently likes some action, such as I do—although the cushiony cloud would have been beneficial to my hemorrhoids.

* * * * * * * * * *

"I don't know what you'd call a wicked city today. Perhaps some tourists seeking the fleshpots of the world could supply the names of a few cities in the Far East or Middle East where women are cheap, gambling crooked, and venereal disease rampant. Yet any names dropped would pale by comparison with the cities of the plains prominently mentioned in the Bible, such as Sodom and Gomorrah.

"According to accounts I have read, the people of these cities lusted from early morn until late night, making Las Vegas a peaceful bluenosed town when comparing one with the other. So terrible was their wickedness that God—according to the Bible—destroyed them by fire sent from Heaven.

"Sodom and Gomorrah were said to be flourishing earlier

than the southern Italian city of Pompeii. Pompeii, lying at the foot of Mt. Vesuvius near Naples, was buried in the year 79 A.D. by volcanic ashes and cinders spouting from a red hot eruption of Vesuvius.

"Archaeologists have splendid records of their excavations, making and confirming history with their finds. But why can't they uncover the ruins of Sodom and Gomorrah and others of the so-branded immoral cities? There's never been a stone unearthed. And these cities weren't even supposed to have been buried like latter day Pompeii, only destroyed by fire.

"If Sodom and Gomorrah had been established cities on any map, they . . . they . . . th . . ." His voice trailed away. He was asleep. I shut off the recorder, my mind intent on what he had said about the Bible: "I only scanned it once."

What a magnificent pretender he was.

When he awoke at precisely four A.M. and called for a martini, I asked, "Do you believe in following the Ten Commandments?"

"I have my own commandments," he answered sleepily. "I don't know how many there are."

"Could I hear them, Woody?" I asked.

He rattled them off:

"Thou shalt have no other gods before me like C.B. De Mille."

"Thou shalt not take the name of the Lord thy God in vain unless you've used up all the other four-letter words."

"Remember the Sabbath Day to keep it holy by blessing yourself while the other hand is in the collection box."

"Honor thy Father and thy Mother, that their days may be long upon the land which the Lord thy God giveth thee, and the tax collector taketh from thee."

"Thou shalt not kill anything less than a fifth."

"Thou shalt not commit adultery unless in the mood."

"Thou shalt not steal—only from other comedians."

* 62 *

"Thou shalt not covet thy neighbor's wife unless she's a beauty."

"Thou shalt not take unto thee any graven image, since I was born one."

"Thou shalt not covet thy neighbor's house unless they have a well-stocked bar."

I should have known better than to have asked him an earnest question. But I tried again: "Do you believe in life after death, Woody?"

"My, you're serious tonight, my little tangerine," he replied between sips of his drink.

"Please, Woody, answer me."

He gulped the remainder of the martini, chewed the olive, and said solemnly, "I only believe in life, Chinaman," and he began reciting:

Though racked with gout in hand and foot,
Though cancer deep should strike its root,
Though palsy shake my feeble thighs,
Though hideous lump on shoulder rise,
From flaccid gum, teeth drop away,
Yet all is well if life but stay.

I never knew who wrote this poem that he dredged up from the recesses of his memory. The next day I made him repeat it and I wrote it down. He maintained he didn't know its origin.

Six

FROM the time I moved in with W.C. Fields until his death, he made the following films: *If I Had a Million*, four Mack Sennett shorts: *The Dentist, The Fatal Glass of Beer, The Pharmacist*, and *The Barber Shop; International House, Tillie and Gus, Alice in Wonderland, Six of a Kind, You're Telling Me, The Old-Fashioned Way, Mrs. Wiggs of the Cabbage Patch, It's a Gift, David Copperfield, Mississippi, The Man on the Flying Trapeze, Poppy, The Big Broadcast of 1938, You Can't Cheat an Honest Man, My Little Chickadee, The Bank Dick, Never Give a Sucker an Even Break, Follow the Boys, Song of the Open Road*, and played a cameo part in *Sensations of 1945*.

Some of these films have been exhumed and brought to public attention by releases in cinema houses, television runs and reruns, and clips on various talk shows—and then are buried again. However, they make very lively corpses, ready to spring back to life on demand.

I had small parts in a few of his pictures, but I was never sure whether I landed them due to our relationship, my talent or looks, or just because he wanted an ally on the set to side with him in arguments. And there were plenty of those.

Many of the gags in these pictures—and large segments of the scripts were conceived and written by Woody—were born while dictating to me or his secretary. If a funny situation hit him just right, he'd laugh until tears ran down his cheeks.

He always went to sleep with a pad and pencil by his bedside in case a comic idea popped into his head. Because sleep came fitfully, his creative juices flowed freely throughout the long nights.

"Any time an idea hits you," he counseled me, "write it down. Don't trust your memory no matter how good you think it is."

"Comedy is a business," he said. "A serious business with only one purpose—to make people laugh. It isn't easy, but pity the poor book and magazine writers, for it's much easier to get a laugh from physical action than from the printed word. Laughs from physical action come from the belly.

"You have to experiment a lot . . . try bits of it out on different people. A cross section, if you can find one.

"An infallible rule I have in comedy is never to break anything. Only bend things. If you shatter a flower pot over some harassing oaf's head, the laughter dies the moment the pot breaks. If you hit him with something that bends, the audience keeps looking at the instrument responsible for the bludgeoning, and the laughs go on. Nothing brittle has any humor. I broke a pool cue once and the house was silent. Next time I got one that looked like iron, bent it, and they went crazy. The best thing to break is a contract."

Woody always believed that the public hated a rich comedian. "If he's rich," Woody reasoned, "he's no longer the underdog. A comic should never move about in public riding in a long car with a liveried chauffeur."

So many people believed he couldn't help being funny, that the moment an audience set eyes on him, they burst into uncontrollable laughter. But any Fields comedy was the end product of strenuous work, with bits of painstaking detail.

"Show me a comic who isn't a perfectionist," he said, "and I'll show you a starving man. You have to sweat and toil and practice indefinitely. A comic should suffer as much over a single line as a man with a hernia would in picking up a heavy barbell.

"A henpecked man gets surefire laughs, but the cardinal rule is that he must triumph over the shrew he married or his harridan mother-in-law in the end, after withstanding attempted bullying and severe tongue lashings. Give him a name that will draw sympathy, like Sylvan Trembleleaf.

"Dress or costume is important. If you are as impeccable as the Prince of Wales, there won't be a snicker in the house. But come out of the wings in some ill-fitting garments, and the audience laughs their heads off. A fat woman can help you out. Every crease, fold and droop of flesh can be the object of hilarity. And oh, yes, you can dress like the Prince of Wales, if you dress only half of yourself that way. For the other half let your baggy pants start to fall or your oversized hat drop over your eyes."

Someone described Woody as "half hobo, half senator." Personally, I think he was, and that had much to do with his success.

"Never test a joke on an Englishman, a Dane, a Norwegian, or a Swede," he advised. "By the time an Englishman solves one, they're already sweeping out the theatre. As for the others, you're lucky to get a trace of a smile for your trouble. Their faces are too frozen from tough winters to crack into happy expressions.

"Always bear in mind that everyone has a percentage of the sadist in him, even though infinitesimal. If I hit you over the head with a club in public, Chinaman, I'd be arrested. In a comedy act, it draws laughter. Comedy is comedy, no matter how implausible. Take those early Mack Sennett comedies, for example. A train roars by a railroad station, and all the men on the platform have their pants jerked off by suction. Impossible? Sure. Laughs? Yes—a million of them. If you have got a good gag, milk it until the blood runs out.

"Or the Keystone Cops: A gang of them starts chasing a wanted man who has run by. But first, they leap a foot into the air and upon descending to the pavement, take up pursuit. See what I mean?"

I said that I did.

"A comedian should quit if he isn't getting any laughs after three years," he went on. "But if he can still make his wife laugh, he'd better stick it out. It's a good sign."

To his contemporaries he was fairly charitable, with the one notable exception of Charlie Chaplin. He referred to him as a "goddamned ballet dancer." It had to be pure jealousy.

Woody once appeared in Superior Court, Los Angeles, to defend himself on a $20,000 plagiarism suit. He wore a red-spotted tie which matched his cherry-hued nose. Harry Yadkoe, a hardware dealer and amateur writer from Newark, New Jersey, charged that when Fields made the picture *You Can't Cheat an Honest Man*, he had used material that Yadkoe had submitted to him in 1938. Through his attorneys Alan Gray and William H. Campbell, Woody denied the charge.

"I won't talk," Woody told reporters. "I might get myself in deeper."

The Easterner claimed that Woody had lifted from him a sequence involving a snake.

Woody came to court carrying a small rubber keg under his arm. Asked what it was, he replied, "Snake medicine, to use just in case of an adverse decision."

Asked specifically what the keg contained, he answered, "It ain't milk."

The jury was treated to an unexpected pleasure: They saw parts of the movie that related to the case. Yadkoe received a judgment of $6,500.

"The moral is," Woody contended, "never have a free movie showing. The audience doesn't always appreciate it."

He drank deeply from the rubber keg. I can only suppose the judge didn't realize it was liquor. Later, Woody appealed the case through new attorneys, and it was denied.

Everyone sent him gags—and even my brother gave him a couple that he used. Sometimes our postman jotted one down on the back of an envelope containing junk mail. But professional writers were deadly poison to him. At a dinner party when Woody was asked, "What's your favorite fish?" he replied, "A piranha in a writer's bathtub." I can't remember him being fond of any of the script-writers he worked with except Bill Morrow, who was knowledgeable in his handling of Woody.

Over and over again, he said to me, "I have no objection to writers preparing my scripts as long as they don't show them to me." He often said that every man on the street thinks he can write comedy, and that if he could, he'd be a pro, but even a pro can't do it satisfactorily. He also claimed that after a number of years all writers begin to look alike. "The world thought the Dionne quintuplets were something extraordinary," he stated. "Well, they're not. A comedy writer is one of a set of thousand-uplets. They're all cut out of the same cloth, and the cloth needs weaving and reweaving. They steal from one another with the abandon of students in a school of crime."

I'm reminded of his experiences with Don Marlowe, one of the "Our Gang" comedy group, who just recently wrote a book titled *The Hollywood That Was*. Woody was auditioning a flock of kids at his Toluca Lake House, along with a director whose name I can't remember. Woody lined up eight children —Marlowe among them—who for some reason were standing at semi-attention, like troops being reviewed. After a cursory inspection of the group, he pointed at Don Marlowe and beckoned him over to a desk where he had seated himself.

Marlowe did as Woody wished and stood prepared to furnish his background, his name, the parts he had played, or perhaps to read a few lines. Instead, Woody filled a martini glass nearly to to the rim with his favorite drink (years later Marlowe said he thought it was water) and handed the glass to him.

"Here's what I wish you to do," Woody instructed. "Run around the room as fast as you can, and hand me back the glass."

Marlowe, somewhat puzzled but obedient, did just that. Woody inspected the glass, turning it around slowly in his hand. Then he showed it to the director. "Not a drop spilled," he said in a complimentary tone. "Did you ever see such talent?"

The director nodded his approval.

"You're hired," Woody told Marlowe, and addressing the other disappointed young actors, he counseled them to go home. Again he turned to Marlowe, got up, patted him on the head and intoned, "What a talent . . . what a talent."

For the next ten minutes Woody explained the type of picture it was, and asked the boy if he could tell jokes. Don admitted knowing several about the farmer's daughter. This made Woody very happy; jokes about the farmer's daughter were becoming such a drug on the market that he was confident none of them would steal any of his thunder.

Don recalls that Woody never had a script, and deliberately used multi-syllabic words that a child actor couldn't understand. Either a kick under a table or a hand dropped on Don's shoulder signalled a cue. If he asked Woody, "Why is a cat's tail like a long journey?" Woody invariably reworded the cue to something like: "Let's see, my son—why is the hindmost part of a feline's body—the extremity known as a tail—like one of the peregrinations of Marco Polo?"

Don's most important job on the set was to run drinks. By this time he knew he wasn't carrying water. His father, Coy Watson, had acquainted him with the facts of Woody's life, as had his school teacher—a well-meaning but puritanical soul who seemed horrified that the boy was breathing the same air in the room with Woody. Don always claimed he was perhaps the world's youngest bartender, at the approximate age of twelve.

He remembers one hot day when Woody wanted ice in his drink, and Don, rushing it back to him, dropped the ice cube. Expecting to be reprimanded and perhaps lose his job, he hung his head and waited for a stream of invectives. "Don't let that bother you, my boy," he heard. "Ice is replaceable." With that, Woody picked up the cube, wiped it off with a silk handkerchief and, dropping it into his glass, remarked, "A little terra firma never hurt anyone."

Don had a few opportunities to watch one of Woody's contemporaries, Wallace Beery, at work, and said that in one respect they were similar: Both would improvise. The difference, though, was that if things weren't running smoothly on the set, Beery often showed his temper and stalked off, but Fields stuck it out, no matter how poor the progress might be.

Woody was an expert at either forgetting his cues or purposely not caring to remember them. It took a real pro to run through a scene smoothly with him, and in order to do this you had to watch his eyes: They were the tip-off that he had finished his lines. If an actor were on his toes, he could make a rush to squeeze in a few lines whenever Woody took a deep breath.

Woody enjoyed getting writers so tipsy that they wouldn't have the foggiest notion of whether or not he was following their lines. Once we were shooting at Chatsworth, in the San Fernando Valley, around a specially-built railroad car. A writer handed Woody a thick sheaf of pages of dialogue. Woody wrinkled his nose in distaste and riffled through them.

"You want me to learn all this, do you?"

"Yes, Mr. Fields," came the answer.

Woody slapped at a fly. "Got the saber-toothed bastard," he mumbled. Then his eyes returned to the script, which he tore into little pieces and tossed into the air. A sudden gust of wind dispatched the typewritten confetti down the tracks. "Breeze from the northwest," he intoned, adding, "A fine day for making moonshine."

If some of his writers are still living after the irritations they went through, it's a miracle. As one of them declared to me, "It's worse than being thrown to the lions to work for him. He can eat a writer alive. The early Christians don't know how lucky they were."

Woody elaborated on this, asserting that he could devour a writing team in seven minutes flat, but claimed they were hard to digest because all those semi-colons and exclamation marks pricked the lining of his stomach.

One of his writers said he had recurrent dreams of a science-fiction nature: monsters from an unknown planet, giant effigies of Woody with fire shooting from their bulbous noses, were invading the earth and destroying anything that happened to get in their way. He maintained that old Fields writers can be recognized on sight, and if lucky enough to escape some of California's mental hospitals, are heard muttering, "My little chickadee . . . my little chickadee."

Every Fields writer learned to his chagrin that the script he had stayed up all night to hone and polish—which he had cut to the bone until only solid laughs remained—was destined to be further amputated by Woody. If a brilliant writer put two or three characters into a scene, Woody threw them out. Dialogue was also severely deleted. If another actor's lines called for him to say, "Egad, what a beautiful day," Woody might cut it to just "Egad."

"No matter what I write," said an exasperated and frustrated Hollywood scripter, "he puts in a pool table."

At dinners Woody sometimes grew verbose knowing he had a captive audience, and would grossly exaggerate happenings that supposedly occurred to him in far-off and generally unheard-of spots in the world. The "Rattlesnake" story from *You Can't Cheat an Honest Man* is a good example.

Smutty stories and jokes with double entendres disgusted him, however. I've seen him walk from the room when talk turned to sex. Speaking on that popular subject, he said, "Sex isn't necessary. You don't die without it—but you can die having it."

* * * * * * * * * *

The day Woody recovered sufficiently from his martini spill to drive to the Paramount Studio on business, my father paid an unexpected call on me.

Ezekial Montijo was a 73-year-old who loved life—a swinger of a senior citizen. He was Spanish and he looked it—proud and fierce. My mother, Carlotta, at that time deceased, had been half Italian, half Spanish. All members of the Montijo family were born in the United States. I inherited my musical fondness from my father, who could play both lively tunes and love ballads on the guitar.

We always got along splendidly. When my first picture, *Ben Hur*, opened in 1926, Poppa sat through it three times, mostly to nudge whatever stranger happened to be sitting alongside him and exclaim pridefully as I came onto the screen, "That's my daughter."

On this day, after a cursory greeting, he began tugging at the ends of his mustache, an unmistakable sign that he had something on his mind.

I was wearing a bowknot pin containing a square diamond with baguettes, a beautiful antique piece of jewelry that Woody had given me. He told me that it had belonged to the Empress Josephine and "now," he said, "after all these years it goes to a Chinaman." I can truthfully say that the jewelry traveled a long, bumpy road from Napoleon, who probably "liberated" it from some conquered country, to Josephine, to Woody, to Nora Bayes (a former actress and girl friend of both Woody and John Barrymore), to Carlotta Monti and—during the years ahead—to the Boulevard Loan Company of Hollywood and back again to Carlotta Monti.

I noticed my father eyeing it.

"Is there something you wish to talk about, Poppa?" I asked, anxious to get at the crux of any problems he might have.

He was gazing at his feet as if he didn't know how to begin. Because he remained silent, I pressed him again. "You have something to say to me?"

After fidgeting with his feet, crossing and uncrossing his legs, he said, "Yes, my daughter. It's—it's about the life you're leading."

"My life is wonderful," I spoke up quickly. "I live like a millionaire with a man I'm crazy about. I have nine servants and keep busy. Who could ask for anything more?"

"There's one more thing you could ask for."

I knew what was coming.

"Marriage," he said.

"Well, now, Poppa, I. . . ."

"You're a mistress," he whispered, making it sound like a dirty word.

I had recently been doing some research on the subject which naturally interested me very much, and the information I had unearthed in the library now enabled me to defend my position.

"Being a mistress," I told my father, "isn't anything to be ashamed of. History has recorded many famous ones." I started naming some: "There was Nan Britton, the paramour of President Warren G. Harding. Why, she even slipped into the White House for clandestine meetings. And then there was Madame Lupescu who practically ran Romania."

My father's eyes had a glazed, sort of out-of-focus appearance. "Let's go back into history," I continued. "What about Madame de Pompadour, the great patroness of eighteenth century French art, or Madame la Comtesse Jeanne Bécu Du Barry, the last mistress of Louis XV of France. She—." Then I remembered that she was guillotined during the Revolution. "Forget her," I advised, and went on: "Lady Hamilton was the illicit lover of Lord Nelson. King George IV of England had a flock of mistresses. And how about Cleopatra, who was the girl friend of Julius Caesar?"

I paused, a little out of breath but proud of my memory, and allowed my library knowledge to penetrate my father's mind. When I heard his reply I knew I'd been unsuccessful.

"Daughter—get married!"

I sighed, and decided to try again.

"In Europe a mistress has a position of solid respectability and is often considered a necessary escape for the jaded married man. A wife may not like mistresses, but has to accept their existence. They wear exquisite clothes and costly jewelry. Years ago they lived virtually in obscurity, tucked away in some small, tastefully furnished apartment near the heart of a metropolis. But today they are out in the open. Mussolini had Clara Petacci who died with him under the machine gun fire of a Communist partisan."

I stopped talking, having run out of history, and waited for his comments.

Again he said, "Daughter—get married!"

Before I could answer, he dragged out a heavy, gold pocket watch on a chain, snapped the lid open, consulted it, whistled in surprise, and said, "I've got to get home. Faranita gets lonesome."

"Who's Faranita?" I demanded.

"Faranita? Faranita?" he repeated.

"Yes, Faranita," I said, certain he had inadvertently let some cat out of its bag.

"She's . . . she's . . . he stammered, avoiding my stare.

"She's what?"

"Well . . . she's my mistress," he admitted sheepishly.

It took about fifteen seconds for the significance of his words to sink in. Why, the old reprobate, I thought. And he came here to censor me!

"How old is she?" I asked.

"Thirty-six."

I was flabbergasted. "Poppa," I said, "how *could* you?"

"My doctor asked me the same question," he replied.

Before I could continue my interrogation, Woody came in, handed his cane to the butler, and I introduced him to my father. "Will you have a drink, Zeke?" he invited.

"Of course," came the ready reply.

"I like that," Woody said, motioning him toward a portable bar. "I can see that you're a man of quick decision, sir. An executive type. Show me a man who won't take a drink, and I'll prove he's part camel." He started mixing martinis.

"Why don't you marry my daughter?" Poppa asked pointedly.

An empty glass slipped from Woody's fingers, shattering against the bar. "This calls for triple strength," he mumbled under his breath, and he made the drink accordingly. "To you, sir," he said, handing one to Poppa. He held his glass aloft as he toasted my father.

"To the coming marriage of my daughter," Poppa proposed much to my chagrin, as he threw his head back and downed the drink.

Woody fixed him another . . . and another . . . and another.

"I'm really a wine drinker, Mr. Fields," Poppa said thickly.

"A wonderful drink, wine," Woody agreed. "It has unexploited values. Did you ever hear of a barefooted Italian grape crusher with athlete's foot?"

No reply came from my father. He was awfully drunk. Woody seemed unaffected. I ordered a taxi for Poppa. He was in no condition to drive, and could pick up his car tomorrow. As I came back from the telephone, I saw Woody with his arm around Poppa's shoulders, and he was saying, "Zeke, my good fellow, I like you. You're a prince of a man. I wonder if I could ask you a favor?"

"Anything for you, Mr. Fields," my father said.

"I wish you'd do me a great honor by marrying my daughter."

"It will be a pleasure," Poppa replied, and asked me, "Which way to the lavatory, Carlotta?"

It was to be the beginning of a lasting friendship.

My father grew increasingly fond of Woody, and vice versa. "He's young in heart and a real character," Woody said, predicting, "But some day he's going to get into serious trouble." His prediction came true sooner than anticipated.

One night a cab brought my father to our house and the driver, supporting his nearly limp body, brought him inside. Poppa's face was black and blue, and he was raving in delirium.

I was nearly hysterical. "I'm going to call your doctor," I told Woody as I rushed to the phone.

"Don't pay him over fifteen dollars," he warned.

My father began muttering, "They tried to kill me . . . they tried to kill me."

"He's dying," I told Woody—after first bargaining with the doctor. "I'm going to call a priest."

"Don't pay him over fifteen dollars," Woody said.

While we waited for the doctor, I put Poppa to bed and telephoned his apartment. A woman answered: It was Faranita. Since she spoke poor English, I told her that I understood Spanish and asked her what had happened. She was reluctant to talk, but I frightened her into all the details by threatening to call the police. She nervously related how her two sons, aged seventeen and eighteen, had come over and found the two living together, had beaten Poppa up and thrown him down a flight of cement stairs.

Of course I had no intention of reporting this to the police, but she became so fearful that her sons would be jailed that, I discovered later, she filed a complaint against Poppa the next day with the district attorney's office.

In the meantime, the doctor appeared. He gave Poppa some

shots, inspected a few body bruises, and patched up his face. Woody handed him the agreed-upon fifteen dollars, and he left.

The doctor had barely gotten out of the front door when Poppa, staggering from the bed, clutched for support at an old-fashioned grillwork clock on the wall and brought it crashing down on his head.

Blood flowed from his right eye.

"Get the doctor again!" I shouted.

Woody ran downstairs, rushed along the portico, and halted the physician just as he was about to reach the street. "Hurry back!" Woody exhorted. "There's been an accident."

The doctor, facing him, said, "This constitutes a separate visit, of course."

"But you haven't left my property," Woody asserted.

The doctor chuckled, believing he had him this time. "Oh, yes I have," he said confidently, and glancing down at Woody's feet, called attention to the fact that he was standing a good six inches into the street.

To the uninformed it could be assumed that Woody was the loser of this tiff, but he proved anything but uninformed: "This, sir, for better or for worse—and in my opinion it's the latter— is a private park. Laughlin Park, to be exact, is bounded by Los Feliz Boulevard on one side and Franklin Avenue on the other. Each home owner or renter is responsible for half the street— for cleaning, paving, and so forth. So you can readily see, sir, that you are standing well within my property."

"All right, all right," the doctor said, giving up the argument and following him to the house, where it took ten stitches to close the cut over Poppa's eye.

While I watched the doctor stitching the wound, the priest arrived, only to have Woody tell him it was a mistake and send him away. I was furious. "This is no time to be tight when my father's dying," I stated.

Woody moved close to the bed, bent low, sniffed, and announced, "He's had too much alcohol to die. That dago red is pumping through his bloodstream like gas going into a car."

He was right. The next day we found out that Poppa had drunk a gallon of wine before the altercation.

A date was set for the hearing on whether Faranita's sons would be indicted for assault and battery.

Woody thoroughly enjoyed all of this. It was an escape from the norm, and part of it had been staged right before his eyes. "I may get La Cava to direct it," he joked.

This was one time I didn't appreciate his humor.

During the next four days Poppa made a speedy recovery. "The old sonofabitch will have to leave soon," Woody remarked. "He's been dipping into my private collection."

"I simply don't believe it," I said indignantly.

"I ought to know," he claimed. "I've got the level of every opened bottle marked, and several have gone down."

"Evaporation," I said.

"Bah," he scoffed, "unless it evaporated in his stomach."

Woody refused to go to the hearing with me. The only time he enjoyed being displayed before the public was on celluloid.

The judge asked Poppa and Faranita their ages. After learning the discrepancy, he said to Poppa, "How dare you molest a woman only thirty-six-years old?"

"I wouldn't exactly call it molesting," Poppa answered.

"I would," stated the judge. "The next time someone finds you living together, you both go to jail."

They never saw each other again.

I recounted the story of the court decision to Woody. He was furious. "Instead of bawling your father out, the judge should have subpoenaed a famous sculptor to erect a statue to him. Anyone as competent as Zeke is in bed at the age of seventy-three deserves something better than a tongue-lashing."

Seven

BEFORE I met Woody I had been studying voice, and I think I might have made it in opera if I had continued. But Woody hated vocalizing with bitter resentment. Many have claimed this feeling came from following singers in his vaudeville days, but I'm inclined to believe it stemmed from his father, who would sometimes haul off and belt him if the boy interrupted during the rendition of a song.

In order to seek a measure of revenge whenever I got angry at Woody, I'd go to my room, close the door, open the windows wide, and release operatic outbursts as the mighty female warrior Brünnhilde from Wagner's *Ring of the Nibelung*. Woody would knock on the door, trumpeting, "Woman, the beams are falling!"

In describing my voice to Will Rogers, he compared it to "the sounds made by a monsoon whistling up an aardvark's asshole."

Once after some minor tiff, I locked myself in my room and began to sing in fine voice. I was reaching the middle of a high note when I heard Woody yell, "Fire!" I broke off in mid-aria, and looked. Smoke was curling from under the door.

Screaming, I unlocked it and ran out, straight into his arms. Aware that I was petrified of fire, he had lit a piece of paper and shoved it under the door.

After the first few romantic years, as we became adjusted to living together, he'd search my room and break my records if I didn't hide them. Concealing them all was difficult, as my collection was an extensive one.

On a day when producer Bill LeBaron came over from Paramount to discuss business, I went to the end of the property, nearly four acres from the house, and in the middle of the pomegranates sang *Ave Maria* at the top of my lungs.

"Who's that singing, Bill?" LeBaron inquired.

Cocking an ear in the direction of my voice, Woody answered, "It's that goddamned crazy Chinaman trying to get a job from you—and if you ever offer her one, you lose me."

That same night a servant knocked on my door to inform me that Mr. Fields wanted to see me in his bedroom. I slipped into a black negligee he admired and applied a few dabs of perfume. To my surprise, there was a stranger in the room with Woody.

"Take off your clothes," Woody ordered.

I looked at the stranger, gasping, "In front of him?"

"This man's a doctor," Woody said.

"But there's nothing the matter with me."

"I hope not," Woody returned, and introduced me. "This is Dr. Patrick. He's going to give you a physical for the insurance company."

Finished, and having passed the physical with flying colors, I asked Woody what it was all about.

"I'm taking out a hundred thousand dollar life insurance policy on you," he explained.

"Who's the beneficiary?" I asked.

"I am. You're a good bet to make me wealthier."

"But I'm healthy. The doctor just said so," I reminded him. "And I'm much younger than you."

He shrugged off this fact. "Age makes no difference. Some

day you're gonna bust something internally, reaching one of those goddamned high notes and then I'll collect a hundred thousand."

* * * * * * * * *

I couldn't count the number of times Woody would say, "Dress up, Chinaman. Tonight we're going to a party." These were pleasant words to hear. I was a gregarious person who loved to socialize. My figure drew admiring glances from the males, and no girl could honestly say she didn't enjoy this optic attention.

On such occasions, Woody dressed immaculately and conservatively. He was the neatest man I'd ever known, showering every evening and tub bathing each morning. Twice daily he changed his shirt and clothing. He always wore a white shirt, custom tailored by a downtown Los Angeles shirtmaker who would send a man out to measure him. Each shirt sported French cuffs, and his favorite cuff links were platinum with sapphires. I picked out most of his haberdashery. His neckties had to be silk, containing red and blue, and he was extremely fond of polka dots.

The cheapest evening accessory he owned was his cane. He refused to carry a malacca or any of the more expensive woods, preferring a plain-ridged bamboo that was seen in many of his comedies.

But even after telling me to prepare to attend a party, we rarely went. An hour later he might call and have me or a servant tell the hostess, "Mr. Fields is suffering from a rare disease he picked up in the Antilles." Periodically he changed the name of the country where he had supposedly become infected.

I got all dressed up the night he said we were definitely going to a party at Earl Carroll's and felt as excited as a schoolgirl going to her first prom.

Carroll lived in Beverly Hills in an all glass-fronted home with sweeping green lawns. Nude girls—wood nymphs with wings—were dancing in the garden as we approached the house. After a penetrating gaze at their nakedness, Woody grabbed my arm.

"Come on, Chinaman," he said. "Let's go home. This is no place for you."

I didn't even get a glass of soda.

It was virtually the same routine at all parties. About going to Edgar Bergen's or Ken Murray's, I remember only entering the house, meeting the host, powdering my nose in the ladies' room—and we were on our way home.

At a Nelson Eddy affair we stayed slightly longer. Eddy was living in director Fred Niblo's house, renting it for himself and his mother. Nelson was a very devoted son. He was also a good friend of mine, a fact Woody resented.

The Niblo home was built of marble. Mrs. Eddy, a woman who exuded much charm, greeted us. "Nelson's in fine voice this evening," she said, beaming at Fields.

Woody muttered some deprecations under his breath that sounded like, "I didn't come here to hear that sonofabitch tear the air to pieces with his tonsils."

"I don't believe I heard what you said, Mr. Fields," said Mrs. Eddy.

Woody muttered, audible only to me, "The old gorgon ought to get an ear trumpet—one she could turn off when her son starts releasing a potpourri of fart-like notes." Then, bowing gracefully before her, he said, "I was paying a compliment to your son's voice."

"Thank you," Mrs. Eddy beamed. "It certainly is pure gold."

Woody whispered to me, "She means fool's gold."

"I'm sure Nelson will favor you with a song," Mrs. Eddy said, as we moved toward the interior of the house.

"The only favor he can do for me is to cut his vocal chords with a stiletto," Woody snarled.

The first voice we heard belonged to an actor who had managed to land a fair part in a movie two years before, and had been at liberty ever since. He was dropping names right and left. They rolled easily off his tongue, and in rapid succession we heard mention of Louis B. Mayer, Lana Turner, Greer Garson, and Bing Crosby. "All good friends of mine," he added.

Before the actor managed to mention another celebrity, a tight-skirted, buttock-swaying starlet wiggled across the room. He followed the undulations of her torso, and gasped, "My God!"

Woody rushed up to him, demanding, "How well did you know *Him?*"

As we circulated around we learned—to Woody's dismay—that every room we entered had a piano, and each piano had a player, and at the piano was a singer.

In the sitting room, Nelson was singing *Indian Love Call*.

"It's too bad the Indians lost," Woody grumbled, "or they'd have burned him at the stake."

Eventually he could stand it no longer. Grabbing two cigarettes from a box, he stuck one in each ear, and ordered, "Find your coat, Chinaman, we're going home." On the way out he thanked Mrs. Eddy—who was bewildered by the cigarettes—bade her goodnight, and said, "We'll come back some time when Nelson's asleep."

* * * * * * * * * *

I never remembered staying at any party long enough to eat anything, but, as Woody told me, "It's better for your figure."

Only once did I ever come close to sampling the food. It was at a lavish party given by Mae West. I was seated next to Woody, Mark Hellinger was on the other side of him, and Dorothy Lamour was alongside of me.

The first course was shrimp cocktail, a favorite of mine, and I was lifting a forkful to my mouth, when he forced it back to the plate.

"Are we leaving?" I guessed.

We were.

Try as he might, Jack Barrymore could never persuade Woody to make the rounds of public drinking places with him. He kept mentioning Perino's, an internationally known restaurant, in the heart of Los Angeles.

"They got Tony Cordero, the best bartender in the world," Jack said. "Tony'll mix you a martini like you've never had before. He knows more about that cocktail than its inventor."

"If I met him coming down the street, would he have an olive in his pocket?" Woody questioned, adding, "That's the supreme test of a good bartender."

Barrymore answered, "Of course not—who would?"

"Carlotta would," Woody said.

Barrymore gave up.

Why Woody even bothered to accept invitations, I don't know. His explanation was, "It's much easier." True, but then he'd always need someone to get him out of what he'd plunged into.

He preferred to do his entertaining at home, and I would act as hostess, planning the dinner and decorations. He insisted on corsages for the ladies. If I gave a Mexican dinner, I'd place red hibiscus surrounded by tiny dainty purple flowers on the table—and so on for other national cuisines.

He ate sparingly at his own dinner parties, picking at some gastronomic delight that might have taken hours of preparation. Even my chicken, which he loved, would only be nibbled at.

Guests didn't stay late at these dinners, and Woody kept a watchful eye for anyone whom he suspected of getting tipsy— at which point that person's drinks would be cut off. He hated drunks.

Some thought this attitude was feigned, or that it was, at best, hypocrisy. He certainly had an enormous capacity for liquor, but the only noticeable effect was on his mind—it became sharper.

"When you woo a wet goddess," he often said, "there's no use falling at her feet."

Carlotta Monti (PHOTO: MAURINE)

Carlotta Monti . . .

W.C. Fields' favorite picture
of her (PHOTO: MAURINE)

"Woody," in his spry middle age

Carlotta wearing one of the "Chinaman" outfits that inspired Fields with his
lasting nickname for her

Fields got his start in vaudeville—as this memento from the Orpheum (Omaha,
Nebraska) attests (RAYMOND ROHAUER)

Fields' first screen appearance—*Pool Sharks* (1915), in which he wore a false moustache and demonstrated the skills he had picked up as a genuine "hustler" (RAYMOND ROHAUER)

This sequence from *The Denti.* (1932) was censored and never shown in regular theatres (RAYMOND ROHAUER)

"Uncle Claude" in 1934 (PHOTO: MAURINE)

Max Asher used to play the same vaudeville and fair circuits as W.C. Fields shortly before World War I. They met again in 1935 as makeup man and star, respectively, in Paramount's *Mississippi* (RAYMOND ROHAUER)

Burns and Allen, "Uncle Willie," and Franklin Pangborn, from a publicity still for *International House* (1932)

Actually, his preference was for entertaining men only. When it was a stag party I'd fade into the background and then sneak up to my room after starting off the festivities. Men were crazy about him. He was a man's man—no doubt of it.

At all-male parties, he enjoyed talking and discussed life in a half-serious manner, running the gamut from hilarity to angry outbursts against conventional customs. He was constantly thrusting at the mores and hypocrisy of society with a sharp-edged tongue which never cut two ways.

Those who had not attended one of his stag dinners usually expected something wild and raucous . . . perhaps a scantily clad dancing girl bursting from a huge cake—but no props or artificial stimuli were needed. It was the people at these dinners who were exciting as they drank the finest of wines and liquors, complimented his flaming desserts, and unburdened their keen minds on a variety of subjects.

Finally tiring of his Encino estate—although he had no valid reasons for it—he decided to move to fashionable Bel Air. Woody always rented. He refused to be burdened by owning a house. I felt sorry for his landlords of the three houses we occupied during the fourteen years I lived with him. It mattered little to him what state of disrepair they fell into. "I won't spend a red cent to fix up someone else's property," he declared.

You might say he ate those words a year before he died. After another move—this time to De Mille Drive—plaster began to crack and peel on the ceiling of an upstairs room. Once or twice, as it flaked from earthquake tremors, it resembled falling snow on a movie set.

Woody called it "very realistic," and commented, "If we weren't living in California, I'd put on my overcoat."

Despite my nagging, he steadfastly refused to have it fixed —until the night he asked me to make him a drink, and I went to the nearest portable bar, which happened to be in the room with the faulty ceiling. In the midst of mixing the gin and vermouth, an idea came to me that was worthy enough, I thought, of being tried on Woody.

Back to him I went, drink in hand, and said, "An awful thing just happened."

"Tell me about it, woman who stirs my sluggish blood," he said.

"As I was in the middle of making the martini," I lied, "some plaster fell into the glass from the ceiling."

He jumped from the chair like it was a hot seat. "Don't just stand there," he ordered. "Phone the plasterer. Tell him to get right over here—and to hurry, so we can avoid another horrendous tragedy."

I willingly obeyed his wishes. The plasterer arrived and did a splendid patch job. When he finished, Woody was very hospitable in his gratitude, and the plasterer got himself plastered.

Hardly had he settled in the Bel Air mansion than he had a severe arthritic attack, most of it concentrated in the joints and resulting in painful inflammation. His body was so sensitive he couldn't be touched anywhere. Edgy and irritable he increased his liquor dosages, hoping they would act as a painkiller.

For a week I hand-fed him.

He scarcely slept, complaining that the silk sheet over him "felt heavy as the metal in a thousand virgins' chastity belts." I went to the Broadway Hollywood and bought a hundred dollars' worth of imported angora wool yarn—each small spool cost one dollar—and I made a blue blanket to cover him. The weight was light, and the heat from his body kept it insulated.

"Has the touch of a cloud," he complimented, pulling it over him. Suddenly his voice rasped, "How much did it cost?"

I told him. With that, he stripped it off the bed, ordering, "Take it back!"

"But, Woody, I paid for it myself," I told him.

In the softest voice possible for him to use, he said, "Could

* 86 *

you pull up my blanket, my devoted Chinaman? It slipped off the bed."

From the same yarn, I made him a blue scarf which he later wore to play golf. He always gambled while playing golf, tennis, or on the putting green, but only with Greg La Cava did he wager large amounts of money. "It's not how well you play the game, but the winning that counts," he averred.

I knew what he meant after an eighteen-hole match with La Cava. He was chuckling, and I never had seen him so happy. "I gave that dago wop a good trimming," he said, "and I owe it all to you, Chinaman."

"To me?"

"Correct, my little bird of paradise. The match was even until the seventh hole. La Cava had an easy putt. But as he stroked the ball, the scarf you made me caught by a sudden, opportune gust of wind, blew in his face. He missed, and from that moment on his game collapsed."

I could understand how such a tense person as La Cava could be upset and thrown off his game. However, there was one point I wanted cleared up: "There was no wind today," I reminded Woody.

"Oh, yes there was," he maintained. "Only a few persons noticed it—namely, La Cava and me. It was a tiny whirlwind, the smallest one I ever encountered since I was lost, drifting helplessly in a catamaran in the Java Sea, and . . . "

"Woody," I cut in, "somehow you managed to make that scarf get in Greg's face, didn't you?"

"You jump at conclusions," he said, "and quite frankly, I do not care to pursue the subject."

I really wouldn't say that he was always trying to gyp somebody, but he did have (and I know this is an understatement) a conniving mind, as none who had the misfortune to deal with him would deny. And lest his mind grow stale from inactivity, he put it to use for sharpening purposes in many petty ways, such as small-time betting in table tennis, tennis, and golf where he shrewdly tilted the odds in his favor.

Woody had a certain select coterie of friends with whom he golfed. It was a tight little group and few outsiders could break in. One tried though. A certain movie bigwig, who must remain nameless, invited him to play.

"Tell Mr. ——" Woody snarled, "that when I want to play with a prick, I'll play with my own."

W.C. Fields' athletic prowess was a topic that was constantly under discussion by his friends. A great debate raged: Was he skillful or just plain lucky? He did not, by any stretch of the imagination, resemble an athlete physically. His stomach protruded, his muscles were noticeably absent, and he seemed reluctant to run for difficult shots in tennis—which could only mean a lack of stamina.

Yet in such contests as golf, tennis and table tennis, he took the measure—and often the cash—of more talented opponents. For one thing, he was vastly underrated. Certainly, at the start of a match, none of his adversaries was fearful or intimidated by a man who sunburned easily, wore a linen cap, a shirt, a sleeveless sweater, and a great gob of white ointment spread on his nose for protection, and carried around a pitcher of martinis. He looked like a real pushover, but Greg La Cava and Jack Mulhall in golf, Humphrey Bogart in table tennis, and Sam Hardy in tennis, discovered they were in error.

Quite often while playing tennis with Hardy, he'd hold a racket in one hand and a nearly-filled martini glass in the other —and he rarely spilled a drop. While serving, he would carefully put the martini down along the baseline, serve, and then pick the drink up again. On several occasions I saw him drop his racket due to sweaty palms, but never his martini glass.

In no sport did he play an aggressive, slashing game that blew opponents off their feet. His technique was to be tricky and aggravating in such a way as to upset his foes and bedevil them out of victory. In tennis he could hit a cross-court shot with so much top spin that when stroked correctly, it drove his challengers into the wire fences. And I often saw him use a reverse English by which the ball, after it landed across the net, would bounce back to his side.

All thought they could beat him at his favorite sports, and it generally cost them some cash to discover they couldn't. Yet they never gave up trying. "Wait until next time" was their favorite cry. When "next time" came, the results were the same. Jack Mulhall used to say, "He's a composite of everything an athlete shouldn't be—but he just keeps on winning."

In a table tennis match against Bogart, Woody reached up under the table and tilted it just as Bogey was about to stroke the little celluloid ball. An irate Bogey netted the ball. "What the hell do you think you're doing?" he demanded.

"Why, nothing," Woody replied, innocently. "It was an earthquake. One of the hazards of California living. This table is squarely over the San Andreas fault."

At another decisive time in the game, when Bogey was leading, Woody sacrificed a possible point by catching a shot in his mouth. Unnerved, Bogey blew six straight points and the match.

La Cava and one of Fields' doctors were often victimized in golf. Playing against the doctor, Woody picked up a handful of loose dirt and threw it into the air, ostensibly to find out which direction the wind was blowing. He learned it was blowing right into the doctor's eyes—who kept blinking, and was playing with only half vision the rest of the round.

"Gave me a slight advantage when he went temporarily blind," Woody told me afterwards.

The president of a San Fernando Valley golf club related the story of a special manhunt that was made for Woody. One day after hooking a long drive he disappeared into the woods with his caddy. "We thought he was lost, for sure," the president said. "After he didn't show up for three hours, we organized a search party, and found him sitting on a tree stump, drinking a martini his caddy had poured from a thermos jug."

"A lovely, sylvan paradise in which to partake of a little refreshment," he commented to the rescuers.

A golfing buddy of his once called someone's attention to Woody's peculiar swing. The other man said, "Forget the swing and concentrate on his waistline."

"He is getting rather heavy," was the reply.

"That's not what I meant," the friend corrected, and he pointed out: "Did you ever notice he never loses a ball and gets penalized? I think it's because he drops one down his pants leg, and suddenly cries, 'There it is!'"

I was a spectator while he played Hardy in a closely contested tennis match. Hardy made what appeared to be a perfect placement that nicked the baseline. Woody went to the approximate spot where the ball had hit, and getting down on his hands and knees for an inspection, called, "Out!"

Hardy was furious. "How can you be so positive on a cement court where no marks are left?" he asked.

Woody reasoned, "There was a large, pregnant ant just behind the line before we played the point. Now the little mother is quite dead, so the ball must have hit her."

* * * * * * * * * *

Six months after recovering from his arthritis he contracted pneumonia and spent nearly a year in the Las Encinas Sanitarium in Pasadena. I stayed in an adjoining room. Most of his friends came to cheer him up and bring him liquor, but Mary Pickford came with chicken soup and Eddie Cantor with roses.

Few friends appeared on weekends. It was during one of these lonesome periods that he said, "Chinaman, you're the only one who gives a damn about me."

His doctor, paying him a visit, advised him to eat a banana a day. "The potassium in a banana is healthful for you," he

stated. At the end of the month this doctor billed Fields for
$250. A few moments after opening the bill, Woody was
served a banana. He picked up the piece of fruit and hurled it
across the room, where it plopped against the wall.

"No banana's worth $250," he said, "not even to a starving
monkey."

After he recovered from his long siege, we went home.
The next day he instructed me to order an ambulance. Baffled,
I said, "You just came home in one. And now you're well.
What do you want another for?"

He explained it was for us to travel to the bank—this way
he would be assured of a smooth ride. At the bank he took
me with him into the safe deposit vault and gave me some
jewelry.

I was very pleased, but not nearly as pleased as when Charley
Beyer told me a few days later that in a conversation he'd
had with Fields, Woody had said, "I love Carlotta best of
all."

* * * * * * * * * *

You can take the girl out of a career, but you can't take the
career out of the girl—and that's the way I felt in 1935. There
are many contagious germs in the world, but none bite with the
ferocity, nor cause the lasting sickness of yearning that the
movies or the stage do. Having once thrust my 7-B shoe into
the cinema door and wedged it open a trifle, I hated to close
it again, regardless of the arguments of Woody who wanted
me as his sole property.

After I won a beauty contest and was crowned "Miss
Hollywood" (and because I think like a woman, the year has
completely slipped my mind!), I thought the door to fame and
fortune would swing wide to admit Carlotta Monti. Not so—
I still had to scramble for parts and take hazardous risks.

I guess the biggest chance I took was when I needed money
to put my sister through high school. I was an extra on the

set while Lewis Milestone was directing *Arabian Knights*, an ancient Academy Award winner starring Mary Astor. A double was needed for Miss Astor.

"Can any woman here swim?" Milestone bellowed through his megaphone.

Stepping forward, I said that I could.

"Fine," Mr. Milestone said. "You get a hundred dollars to jump off a boat near Long Beach in Arab clothing. The water is deep and cold."

I stated I was agreeable.

"And," Mr. Milestone reminded, "pretend to drown."

I said a little prayer and jumped, and when they hauled me aboard, Mr. Milestone complimented, "Very realistically done. You actually seemed to be drowning."

I gasped, "I was. Actually I can't swim a stroke."

Still another time, in a Ken Maynard picture, they were looking for a woman who could ride a horse and take a fall. Of course I spoke up, claiming I was a veteran horsewoman. I had never been on a horse—or bet on one—or even ridden a merry-go-round. The ground just seemed to rush at me in all my tender places. It was a painful experience, leaving me aching and bruised.

I received a phone call that M-G-M was interviewing hundreds of girls for a dancing part in a forthcoming picture called *Robin Hood of the Eldorado*, to star Warner Baxter and Margo, with William A. Wellman directing and John Considine, Jr., producing. The plot revolved around the famed California bandit Joaquin Murrieta.

"But what chance would I have against so many other girls?" I asked.

"An excellent chance. It's for a Spanish gypsy number, and in my book you qualify."

That decided me. I went for an audition. As I was wildly dashing up and down the stage in a fire dance number, I heard Chester Hale, the choreographer, exclaim, "That's the girl!"

I got the part.

There was only one hitch. The film was scheduled to be shot near a village called Strawberry, high in the Sierra Nevada Mountains, in Tuolumne County. Woody kicked like a steer when I broke the news.

"If you go, don't bother to come back," was his angry retort. "Stay up there and live with the mountain lions."

I went anyway. The company set up location deep in the wilds. I'd often heard the expression "in the bosom of nature," and here I was dead center in it. We lived in tents, each with a stove in the middle, and generated our own electricity.

On the fourth day I developed a raging fever. Members of the cast kept their distance from me, thinking that whatever I had was something highly contagious. I didn't know at the time, but I was the victim of a tick bite—a poisonous tick had infected me with something diagnosed by the medical profession as Relapsing Fever. I believe it's related to Rocky Mountain Spotted Fever. The illness causes recurrent periods of fever, chills, headaches, and neuromuscular pains, each lasting from five to seven days.

I managed to telephone Woody, gasping out the news.

He was deeply worried. Being a man who had no "I told you so's" in his system, he didn't take me to task for my disobedience.

"Whatever you've got, don't scratch anything," he counselled. "I'm going to send Della up to bring you back."

He promptly chartered a plane, which flew to Sonora, the nearest airfield. He then hired an ambulance to drive thirty miles to Strawberry.

Della arrived, and to my surprise, was accompanied by my sister, Eloise. When we landed in Los Angeles, another ambulance was waiting to rush me to the hospital, where Woody had sent doctors to examine me.

"You're only the fifty-ninth person in California to contact Relapsing Fever," said one of my seven doctors, who was the husband of Mary Astor.

Woody, still sulking over my leaving him, refused to see me. Instead, he sent Sam Hardy for daily reports. I'm always overly dramatic, and in confidence I told Sam, "I'm dying."

Of course it wasn't quite that serious, but I did lose weight until I was only skin and bones. Newspaper photographers wanted to take my picture, and I refused.

At last Woody visited me. He pulled a chair close to the bed and held my hand, and in a voice sounding like an alley cat with asthma, said, "Chinaman, did I ever tell you about the time I caught mobeyjawbuss in the New Hebrides? I was in traction for . . ."

"Oh, Woody," I said, my voice trembling and tears filling my eyes, "I love you very much."

He disliked emotional women, so changed the subject rapidly, asking, "What kind of a part did you have?"

"I was the bandit's woman."

He smiled and declared, "Well, you're my woman now, and maybe the role won't be much different. A lot of theatre owners and studio executives have called me a bandit."

I started crying again. I was very happy.

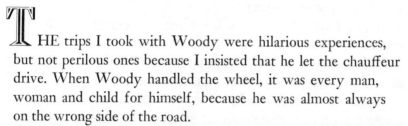

Eight

HE trips I took with Woody were hilarious experiences, but not perilous ones because I insisted that he let the chauffeur drive. When Woody handled the wheel, it was every man, woman and child for himself, because he was almost always on the wrong side of the road.

"Dratted maniacs," he called all other drivers. "They've got a personal vendetta against me."

Women, in particular, were the bane of his driving existence. He believed that they should be permitted behind the wheel only during certain hours of the day, on specially assigned streets, and not be allowed to carry passengers; and that it ought to be a felony if they were caught driving at night. "No doubt exists that all women are crazy," he maintained, "it's only a question of degree."

On our first trip, which was only to Santa Barbara, a stretch of ninety miles of beautiful seacoast, he decided to use the Cadillac, a 16-cylinder job equipped with fresh flowers in a vase, an electric outlet for drink mixing, a lap robe, a speaking tube to the chauffeur, and a portable icebox. He was infatuated with iceboxes. Many times he was more solicitous of its welfare than of mine. And if I sound like a spurned woman, I was. He either carried a portable icebox with him in the car, or shipped one by train to his destination, the charge often coming to more than if he had bought a new one on arrival.

"It provides the perfect temperature for housing my olives and onions," he justified. "They deserve the best."

For the Santa Barbara excursion he had a special map enlarged and thumbtacked onto the garage wall. With a pointer in his hand—the kind schoolteachers use on blackboards—he plotted the trip before the amazed face of his chauffeur. He reminded me of a field marshal of some foreign army charting invasion routes during a briefing for his officers.

He discoursed at great length, citing certain cities through which we would journey, such as Santa Monica, Oxnard, Ventura. Finished, he turned toward the chauffeur. "Is everything clear, Sam?"

The chauffeur replied, "Certainly, sir. Nothing to it. Just hit the coast highway and stay on it to Santa Barbara."

When the chauffeur left, Woody snarled to me, "Remind me to get rid of that know-it-all bastard. He makes everything seem too easy."

On one of our exploratory drives around Los Angeles and environs, we decided to see Big Tujunga Canyon, a quiet mountain road dotted with horse corrals and thickets of dwarf evergreen oaks. We first motored through Glendale, then Montrose and finally joined the canyon road.

We reached our destination just before darkness descended, and Woody ordered the chauffeur to swing the car around and head for home. It had been a beautiful excursion and I felt saddened that it was over.

Suddenly the mountains shut out the last of the dusk, and darkness was upon us. With the arrival of night it was a little confusing to retrace our route, and the chauffeur conveyed his perplexities to Woody.

"Nothing to it," Woody replied confidently. "Just follow my instructions."

At four consecutive intersections he ordered, "Turn right."

He had been drinking more heavily than usual, and I was certain he was confused. I told the chauffeur to stop at an oil station where I inquired the way to Glendale.

"Turn right," the operator advised.

Defeated, I shrugged, and from then on let Woody handle things. After he bellowed for a couple more right turns, we found ourselves back on a familiar road in Glendale, and I have to admit that the mileage back was less than our original foray.

"Woody," I said, "if someone gave you a road map and wanted to go to Las Vegas, you'd end up in Alaska. How come you knew this road so well? Have you been over it before?"

"Didn't know it at all," he snickered. "Never even heard of it."

"Well, then," I demanded, "how did you manage all those correct turns?"

Clearing his throat, he laughed cacklingly and said, "I simply know that if you keep turning right you get into less trouble than going left."

For a single day's outing, Woody would usually pack the trunk of the car with foodstuffs from gourmet markets—delicacies like pâté de foie gras, tins of lobster, crab, caviar, and anchovies—buying enough for twenty people. Such over-buying was probably due to his ever-hungry childhood.

He wasn't very talkative while motoring—he simply mixed drinks and peered from the window. If the scenery became really majestic, a heavy silence hung over him. I think he was actually awed by the wonders of nature, although he wouldn't admit it. "I remain silent so that I can hear the flowers grow," was his excuse.

We traveled to Arizona several times, always to Phoenix; to the Coronado Hotel across from San Diego; Soboba Hot Springs; San Francisco; and the beach nearby at Malibu.

During my years with Woody he kept looking for Indians the moment we crossed the Arizona line. He always expected to sight wild Indians in that state, but never even saw one in front of a cigar store. Indians of any tribe—they were all the same to him—were one of his pet aversions. He kept thinking they were holding tribal meetings for the single purpose of scalping him and filling his body with arrows. Of them he said, "If the redskins were organized into one federation and had more firewater, they'd still own the U.S., and General Motors would be selling buffalos instead of cars."

He was also apprehensive of the Chinese. "All they have to do is give each one a gun, plus a few rounds of ammunition, and they could conquer the world," he said. "It may happen some day." And "If they can't do it by brute force, they can accomplish it by cleverness. All they have to do is shrink the neck size of customers' shirts at every laundry, and everybody will choke to death."

He was very obliging when kids asked him for autographs, but occasionally, if the child didn't fully release the paper he was signing, he would scrawl part of his signature over the holder's fingers or hands.

He was often hostile, though, toward mothers who requested an autograph for their children. "Out of my way, old crone," he cried to one persistent woman. "You should be ashamed of yourself for having a child at your age."

In San Francisco, he left a woman with eyes bugging. He had given her an autograph and then politely inquired about her offspring. The woman said pridefully, "He's a tough little one."

"Madam," Woody commented, "there's no such thing as a tough child—if you parboil them first for seven hours, they always come out tender."

Asked if he believed in the adage, "Children should be seen and not heard," he shook his head in disagreement and responded, "I believe children should neither be seen nor heard from ever again."

He took several trips with men only—notably Westbrook Pegler and Greg La Cava. Both excursions were to Phoenix. Martini in hand, he woke La Cava up at five-thirty in the morning to watch the sunrise over the desert from their hotel room.

"Early to bed, early to rise, makes a man healthy, wealthy, and wise," he informed the sleepy-eyed director.

"You're all three of those already," La Cava growled.

Woody thought over his friend's words, then said, "You know, Greg, you're right," downed his martini, and hopped back into bed.

For Pegler he had great admiration. "Anything I damn, he's glad to damn," he said, summing up the attitude of the columnist. They really had something in common: both were angry men.

The person who traveled with Woody more than anyone was his New York agent, Billy Grady, who later served as casting director for M-G-M Studios. Grady—a gregarious and garrulous, cocky, two-fisted Irishman—represented and associated with some of the most famous people who trod the boards and appeared in motion pictures. After twenty years of agenting on a no-contract basis, no actor or actress owed him a cent—with the exception of Woody, who promised payment by saying he was remembering Grady in his will.

The two had traveled together before I met Woody, but stories of their trip to Florida, where Woody was to make a Paramount picture called *It's the Old Army Game*, with Eddie Sutherland directing, were so often recounted that I could tell them in my sleep. To me they were priceless.

Woody was then with his current heart throb, a southern girl he called "Putsie," whose specialty—among other accomplishments—was puffing on long cigars, and he insisted Grady accompany them.

"We'll motor," Woody suggested, "and inhale the glorious scenery on the way down from New York."

Grady had little choice in the matter. Fields owed him considerable money in back commissions, and he had to protect his investment from either getting killed or standing trial for murder, as in those days it was Woody's custom to carry a heavy-headed cane and lower it on the cranium of anyone who might best him in an argument. If Grady brought up the subject of his delinquent agent's commissions, Woody waved it aside by saying, "Didn't I tell you you're taken care of in my will?"

"You may outlive me," Grady kept reminding him.

"Nonsense, my good man," Woody would retort, "I'm already pre-embalmed from all the liquor I've drunk."

If General Sherman thought he encountered resistance marching through the South during the Civil War, his difficulties were child's play compared to the irritations Woody and party faced.

The agent did the driving, in an open Lincoln touring car. Woody and Putsie sat in the back seat smoking extra-long cigars. The comedian ordered frequent stops to sample the refreshments he had stashed in the trunk. He refused to pour from a bottle while the car was moving, his explanation being, "I wouldn't risk spilling a drop of our precious cargo."

Woody and Putsie appeared to be unusually fond of each other, but were never seen to embrace publicly. But then, how much closer than two cigar lengths could they get to each other?

The travelers became lost on a lonely dirt detour somewhere in the Georgia woods, and the gas gauge had dropped to zero. Ahead they spotted a dusty, one-pump gas station. They stopped, and waited for the attendant. Grady leaned on the horn. No one appeared. In the rear seat Woody pulled himself to his feet, waved his cane in the air, and began thundering invectives that threatened to defoliate the trees for miles around. "Anyone around to run this goddamned thing?" was his final sentence.

From high on a hill house porch a bearded man, rocking in a chair, shouted, "I run the goddamned thing, why?"

"We need some gas," Woody trumpeted.

The bewhiskered figure never broke his rocking cadence. "How much?"

"Does it make any difference?" Woody demanded.

"Well, mebbe I ain't got that much," the voice floated down.

Woody cried, "Just give us what you have."

The rocking continued. "I need some for myself," the porch sitter decided.

Woody's face became an apoplectic hue. He raved and ranted. Putsie tried to soothe him. The stubborn rustic in the rocking chair was one of *her* people. She addressed Woody by her pet name. "Now, Pokey, listen to your Putsie. These people down here move slow. You got to give them time."

"I'd like to give *him* time," Woody roared, adding, "either in Sing Sing or Alcatraz." Once more he took charge. "Do we get gas or not? If we don't, we'll go somewhere else."

"Where'll you go, brother?" the man asked, rocking complacently.

Woody retorted, "If you were my brother I'd see to it the family decreased by one."

"Where'll you go?" the man repeated.

"Oh, we'll find somewhere."

"You-all will hafta ask me, and I ain't of a mind to tell you."

Believing a stalemate had been reached, Grady entered the discussion. "See here, sir, we need gas to get to Florida. Will you please sell me just enough to get us to another station?"

"Well . . ." the man mulled it over a full minute. "All right, I'll give some to you, young feller, but that Yankee in the back seat I don't like none."

He slowly rose from the rocker, stretched his bony frame, and stood surveying the scene at the bottom of the incline, complaining, "Have I gotta walk that hill and back again?"

"If I get my foot against your ass, you'll come down like a falling star and go back up like an airplane," Woody said.

Slowly the man descended, looking like an Alpine climber picking his way safely down a precipitous slope. It was now a full half hour since the motorists had stopped at the pump. From his pocket, the man pulled a bunch of keys that must have numbered a hundred. He tried about two or three dozen before he found the correct one and unlocked the pump. Woody was seething, and Putsie was placating him.

The man was glaring at the actor as if he wanted to strangle him, and Woody was returning the glare with the same intent in mind. The man began to pump the gas.

Putsie whispered something to Woody and he, in turn, said to Grady, "Ask the sonofabitch if there's a ladies' room around here." Grady obeyed, nodding his head toward Putsie.

The bearded rustic scratched his chin. "What's that thing you want?"

"Have you got a toilet for a lady?" Woody barked.

The man bellowed back at him, "What's she want to do?"

Anger was mounting again in Woody. The veins in his neck swelled. He could have been heard all the way to Atlanta as he amplified his voice. "Whaddya mean, what's she want to do? She wants to go to the toilet!"

"She does, huh." The man nodded in understanding. "Well, let her do what everybody else does around these here parts. She can go in the bushes, or she can climb the hill to the outhouse. Most folks use the bushes."

Woody threw up his hands, exasperated. "Well, that's just dandy. Any particular bush you had in mind, mister?"

The gas attendant didn't answer. With all of his pumping, not a pint of gas had gone into the tank. An hour had dragged by since they rolled up to the station. Finally, a thin stream began trickling through the hose. Putsie headed for the bushes, mumbling something about snakes.

"Keep smoking," Woody called after her. "It'll choke the slimy creatures." Then he began hurling some unprintable words at the rustic manning the pump, concluding with, "Hurry up, you country bumpkin, and let us get the hell out of here!"

The man shut off the gas pump. "Just for that language, mister," he reproached the actor, "you ain't gonna get no more." He pointed at Woody. "You and that lady in the bushes can get outta here jest soon as she's finished."

Grady pleaded with the man, but he refused to pump another drop. The Lincoln had received three gallons. The bill came to forty-two cents and Grady handed the operator a five-dollar bill. He examined the currency, holding it up in the sunlight, looked piercingly at Grady, at Woody, and at Putsie, who had returned. Grumbling something about "gettin' some change," he began a slow climb up the hill.

Grady suggested to Woody that they leave, to save time.

Woody shook his head resolutely. "I'll give that old bastard nothing," he snarled.

They waited, and the man came wearily down the hill. He was a dollar short. Grady glanced appealingly at Woody.

"Get the dollar!" he ordered.

The man slowly shuffled up the hill again, descended still more slowly, and handed them the change in nickels and pennies. To secure three gallons of gas it had taken an hour and twenty-two minutes, plus a rip in the side of Putsie's dress where it had been snagged on a bush. Her thighs stung from insect bites and scratches.

They drove off.

Just around the bend of the road was one of the largest and

most modern gas stations they had seen since leaving New York.

"Stop the car," Woody ordered. "This calls for a giant sampling of the grape."

Grady said that for the first time since he had known his client, Woody didn't need an excuse to engage in his favorite pastime.

That evening they registered at a small-town hotel. The dilapidated edifice was a two-story affair, with no fire escapes —the kind of a place that looked like a harbor for rats.

What first greeted the eye, as they entered a paper-thin-walled room, was a "thunder mug" in the open door of a commode. Over it hung a sign: TOILET AND BATH— DOWN THE HALL. Grady's room was a rear cubbyhole, and Woody and Putsie were quartered in front rooms.

Grady didn't get much rest. The mattress was filled with cornhusks which creaked loudly when he turned over. At about two in the morning, when sleep finally came to him, he was awakened by the baying of hounds under his window. As there was no telephone in the room, he went to the second floor landing to call to the night clerk.

"I can't do nothin' about it, Mister," the clerk answered sleepily. "Those dogs belong to the police, and the station's next door."

Grady could well imagine what torture Woody was going through. Most dogs seemed to be his enemies, and in the past some had been tempted to exercise their teeth on his shinbone.

In the morning the agent knocked on his door, and went into his room to inquire how he had slept. Woody shook his head. "Terrible," he said. "The corn nearly killed me. Kept me awake all night."

Grady was aware that his client would sample any kind of liquor, but wondered where he had gotten hold of a jug of corn liquor. He knew there was none in the car, and he hadn't seen him buy any. Thinking of the distilling speed in the

Deep South, he remarked, "The corn must have been too new."

"Too new, hell," Woody returned, "I've had it on my big toe for a week."

From the adjoining room, Grady heard a weird medley of sounds. "What in the devil is that?" he asked.

"Putsie," Woody said. "She's the only woman born in America who can't speak English but can snore in seven languages."

Woody and Grady were a grumpy pair that morning, and their mood was compounded by finding a flat tire on the Lincoln. Not only couldn't they locate the key to the spare tire lock, but the only garage in town that could repair the flat was closed, with a sign outside: GONE FISHING.

Stopping a man approaching on the street, Woody pointed to the sign on the garage, and asked, "How long does that mean?"

"Depends on the wind," the man said.

Woody wanted to know what the wind had to do with it. "If it's from the west," the man explained, "means the bass are bitin' and there's no tellin' when he'll be back. If it's from the east, they ain't hittin' and he won't stay long."

Digesting this, Woody asked, "Suppose it's from the north or south?"

The man stiffened and became belligerent. "You bringin' the Civil War into this talk?" he demanded.

"I'm just bringing the wind," Woody said quickly. "Which direction is it coming from today?"

The man wet his thumb and extended it over his head. "West."

"That means he may be gone a long time?"

"That's the way it is," the man returned.

Abandoning hope for fixing the tire locally, Grady telephoned the nearest town—twenty-eight miles away—and the repair man arrived two hours later. A local locksmith took an additional forty minutes to free the spare.

The turn of events ignited Woody into a castigating mood, one which persisted throughout the day. Eventually they hit the road again, this time with Putsie behind the wheel and Woody and Grady dozing in the back seat.

Suddenly the car stopped with a jerk and the motor died. To their horror, they found themselves wedged over a railroad track, stranded on a rustic one lane road in the middle of typical "Tobacco Road" country.

Recovering from his lethargy in a hurry, Woody yelled at Putsie, "What the hell are you doing on this godforsaken road, anyway? What's wrong with the car? A train may be coming! Goddamnit, do something, somebody!"

Putsie shrugged, and pushed down hard on the starter. There wasn't a sound. She calmly lit a cigar, after first biting off the end and spitting it out the window.

Jumping from the car, Woody began running around in short circles, ordering, "Get out, all of you! Hey, Grady! Go down the track and flag down any train. Putsie, you go the other way and do the same thing. If either of you see anybody, from a Neanderthal to a midget, ask him for help."

It was oppressively hot. Grady removed his shirt to signal any approaching train, and sprinted away. Putsie began running in the opposite direction. After a hundred feet, she stopped and turned toward Fields.

"What's the matter?" he wanted to know.

"I've got nothin' to wave."

"Wave your ass like you do in front of men," he advised.

Putsie was miffed. "Now, Pokey . . ." she began.

"Take off your dress!" the comic interrupted. "Take off your panties! Take off anything—and wave it!"

Discussing the situation with me years later, Woody said he wasn't quite sure which direction he hoped the train would come. He was positive that if the engineer saw Putsie half naked, he'd come to a quick stop, and the car and contents would be saved. As for Grady, the sight of his semi-nude body wouldn't stop a train; and if he got run over, Woody's worries of paying commissions would be ended.

Lifting the hood of the Lincoln, he began tinkering with the motor. Grady found out later that he used a corkscrew, an item Woody once claimed was "the finest precision instrument ever invented." Giving up after muttering, "I always wondered what a spark plug looked like," he raised his head, glanced up toward the sloping bank of land, and saw a typical Georgia cracker staring at him over a rail fence. The man was holding the reins of a pair of horses attached to a plow.

"In trouble?" the onlooker politely inquired.

"Trouble?" Woody snorted. "That's the silliest goddamned question I ever heard. Certainly I'm in trouble. Do you think I stopped in this place because I'm a nature lover? Is there a train due along here?" he asked anxiously.

The farmer reached into his overalls pocket, extracted a heavy nickel-plated watch, snapped the case open, studied it, and scrambled down the bank.

"About time for the 4:48," he calmly announced.

Up the track a winded Grady stopped running, turned around and saw Woody removing articles from the car. True to tradition, the first thing he unloaded with loving care and placed out of harm's way in soft grass, was the booze. Next he hauled forth traveling bags, clothes, a typewriter, and a case of invaluable camera lenses recently brought from Germany to be used in shooting his next picture.

He then began screaming like a banshee at the stranger.

The man stood in the middle of the tracks and swung his head right and left. Wetting a forefinger, he touched the tracks. Not satisfied, he knelt and laid his ear flat against the steel rail. "Yup—she be a-comin'," he announced.

A shouted message to Putsie and Grady brought both of them, breathless, back to the car. Woody commanded everyone to retreat to the safety of the bank. Turning to the farmer, he asked, "Can't you get those goddamned horses of yours to pull us off?"

The man shrugged.

"By the way," Woody said, "which direction does the train come from?"

"What's the difference?" was the laconic comment. "You gonna get hit anyway."

A stream of curses followed. "Give me an answer: Will those goddamned horses pull us?"

"Wal, it'll take a little time." The answer came slowly. I gotta take the animals down to the gate to get 'em through."

"Everything in this miserable country takes time. Where's the gate?"

"Down the road a piece."

"How far down the road?"

"A fur piece."

Woody was using great restraint to keep from exploding. "You talk like it's in the next county."

"It is," the man replied.

"Oh no, oh no, oh no," Woody mumbled despairingly, as he was forced to ask the obvious question of how far was the next county.

"Only quarter of a mile," the man answered.

Woody spat out a volley of oaths, and said in an aside, "You've got to be a linguist to understand these foreigners." Then an idea seized him. "The hell with that! Rip the goddamned fence down!"

"Wal, I dunno," the man said, dubiously.

"This is an emergency—a matter of life or death," Woody pressed him.

The farmer stated, "I don't think my boss, Mr. Abernathy, would 'preciate me tearin' down his fence."

Woody hammered on the fender of the Lincoln with his cane. "The hell with Mr. Abernathy! I'll square things with the old bastard."

Placing a finger over his lips, the man cautioned, "Don't talk like that about Mr. Abernathy, Mister, he's our preacher."

"I wouldn't care if he's the product of immaculate conception," Woody retorted. He reached into his pocket. "Here," he said, handing the man a twenty-dollar bill.

As the farmer pocketed the money, Woody ran up the bank ahead of him, to the fence. Stubbing his toe, he discovered he didn't have his shoes on. Curses filled the air.

"Mr. Abernathy wouldn't like that swearing, Mister," warned the farmer again.

Woody ignored the remark. With a mighty effort, he removed the two top rails, leaving the lower one. The horses, when he yelled, "Giddap!", started through the opening. One made it but the second balked. The horse that got through turned around, facing the second one, fouling the harness. The man came to Woody's aid, and between the two of them, managed to bring the animals down to the car.

Rummaging in the trunk, Woody found a tow chain and handed it to the farmer. "Hitch it to the car!"

"To the front or rear?" the man asked.

"What the hell's the difference? Goddamn it, just hurry!"

The chain was fastened to the rear axle, but before moving the horses the man knelt down before the tracks, pressed his ear to the rail, and informed, "Here she comes."

Woody jumped into the car and got behind the wheel to steer it. Grady and Putsie stood alongside. "For Christ's sake, get moving!" he commanded the farmer.

The farmer kept staring at Putsie.

"What is it now?" Woody asked.

The farmer said, "I ain't never seen no woman smokin' a cigar before."

"Have you ever heard of one being jammed up a man's ass?" Woody asked him.

"Wal, no," the man replied.

"You're not only going to hear of it, but experience it in

about ten seconds if you don't get moving," came the warning.

The horses strained, and the big car gradually moved off the tracks. After tethering the horses, the farmer came back to the car. For the first time he noticed Putsie's ample breasts hanging partially out of her dress from bouncing along the tracks, and her panties, that were to be used for flagging down the train, in her hand.

The farmer covered his eyes with the palms of his hands, muttering, "Mr. Abernathy wouldn't like it."

"If he's human he would," Woody said.

Searching in the grass where he had cachéd the liquor, the actor located a bottle of brandy, took a huge swig, wiped his mouth with the back of his sleeve, and asked, "By the way, my good fellow, is the train that's almost due a passenger or a freight?"

"I dunno," the man replied, "I never seen it. I live over in the woods and only heerd the whistle."

Woody took another pull at the bottle, lowered it, spat contemptuously, and said, "Well, I'll be goddamned if you're not the stupidest sonofabitch I ever had the displeasure of meeting."

"Zat so?" the man returned. "Wal, I ain't so goddamned stupid that I let me car get stuck plumb in the middle of a railroad track."

With that parting sally, he led his team of horses away.

Woody and Putsie laughed, and the comedian said to Grady, "You know, Billy, I like that rural hayseed sonofabitch."

A cloud of dust appeared down the road and a car unable to squeeze past sounded its claxon. The car had Georgia plates. The driver, a young man in his twenties, alighted and Grady explained their predicament. The fellow nodded, performed some magic under the hood, got in, stepped on the starter, and the motor purred like a kitten.

Woody smiled broadly. "Thank you, kind rescuer of

distressed wayfarers. We had a pretty narrow escape. The train due at 4:48 must be late."

"No," came the answer, "she's not late. She went through on time, only not through here. This is a storage track. Hasn't been used for over a year. The main line is over about a mile."

Woody offered the bearer of this news a drink. He declined, and the others reloaded the Lincoln. Woody slipped in behind the wheel. As they drove away, he spotted the farmer and his horses around the bend, slowed the car, and yelled, "What I said about liking you doesn't go. You're still a stupid sonofabitch." And they were off for Florida.

Nine

WITH no provocation, Woody was growing increasingly jealous of me, almost pathologically so. When I accompanied him to the studio I could hardly talk with any man on the lot. Even a friendly "hello" aroused his suspicions. He would immediately scowl and ask, "Who's that pimp?" On the set he wanted me close to him. Even Henry Hathaway, the director, was suspect, and he was a friend of many years.

However, Woody's flareups didn't bother me too much because they were the acts of a man in love.

A little scheme that he concocted had me fooled for nearly a year. He kept saying, "My little chickadee, you need a house of your own . . . something to remember me by after I'm gone." And he would send me house hunting. I'd find some darling, modestly-priced places and take him around to inspect them. But when it came to down payment and escrow time, he backed off with a thousand excuses—and none of them was "I can't afford it."

His objective was to keep me busy all day so that he'd know of my whereabouts. Once he even checked on me in a ladies' room by sending in a strange woman, who said, "There's a man outside with a cane—sort of fat with a funny nose—and he wants to know what you're doing in here."

I was furious. "You tell the fat man with the cane and the funny nose that when a woman has to go, she has to go, just like a man has to." My grammar was imperfect, but I knew that he'd get the message.

Movies were one of my loves, but I could seldom get Woody to leave the house to see one. In his favor, let me say that unlike numerous egotistical Hollywood stars, he had no projector, no miniature theatre in his home for screening his old movies over and over again, *ad nauseum.*

If I went to a movie alone, he might call me a liar upon my return and accuse me of a rendezvous with some man. Once, to test me, he said, "Tell me about the picture, my woman of low cunning."

Keeping my temper under control, I said, "Boy meets girl. They fall in love. They have problems. They get rid of problems. Boy proposes to girl in moonlight. Girl accepts. They kiss and fadeout."

"Your powers of retention are remarkable," he observed.

At one time for a couple of days I had a strange, creepy feeling that I was being followed. Although I didn't actually see anybody constantly behind me, it was something I sensed. Then I became convinced I'd been right in my assumptions. I discovered that everywhere I drove, when I glanced in the rear view mirror, I would see the same car a couple of hundred feet behind. I tried to lose it by going through light signals at the very last second, but somehow that car managed to stay with me. At first I was frightened, then I realized what was happening: Woody had put a private detective on my trail.

After making him promise not to tell Woody that I knew, I consulted Gene Fowler. I learned from him that it was a customary practice for Woody to have his girl friends followed —and Gene related the one time Woody's plans had come a cropper.

When Woody first came to California, he was a pal of Tex Rickard, the illustrious sports promoter. The pair cut dashing figures in their open Phaeton cars. They imported girl friends from New York, and in order to stash them in a locality that was convenient yet far enough for them not to have any interference from other men, they sent them to the Saugus ranch of William S. Hart, which was unoccupied at the time. (Later it was made into a museum containing the film cowboy's memorabilia.)

Woody proposed that he and Rickard hire detectives to keep close tabs on the girls, which would more or less curtail any outside activities. The two detectives employed were young and personable, and highly susceptible to the charms of the Eastern showgirls.

On one of Woody's and Rickard's periodic visits to the ranch, Woody started to embrace his girl, who halted him with the cry, "Don't touch me . . . don't touch me!"

The comic stepped back, peered at her, and inquired, "Is it leprosy or loose bowels?"

"Neither. It's a husband," came the reply. "My girl friend has one too."

Both girls, they learned, had married their detectives.

In an angry mood, the jilted actor telephoned the detective agency and castigated them together with their two employees who he claimed had "betrayed and broken faith with the contract." Calling them Judases, he demanded his and Rickard's money be returned. A satisfactory settlement was agreed upon.

* * * * * * * * * *

I continued to see the same car behind me. I couldn't shake it off. It had become a sort of game, in which I was the hunted. I drove to Beverly Hills to see a girl friend. The weather was miserable, wet, and chilly. As I parked outside the apartment, I saw the detective's car slide into a place halfway down the block.

I hurriedly walked to his car. He quickly picked up a

newspaper, pretending to be engrossed in reading. Opening the door of the car, I said, "I know you're following me."

He looked sheepish and lowered the paper.

"Do you have any heat in the car?" I asked.

He shook his head.

"Listen," I proposed, "why don't you drive somewhere where it's warm, and come back here in exactly two hours. I'm just going to see a friend," and I added, "a lady friend, and if you're not here when I come out, I promise to wait for you."

He was agreeable.

Two hours passed. I left the apartment, and there he was. He looked half frozen. I guessed, "You've been here all this time."

"Yes," he answered.

"Why didn't you do as I suggested?"

He said, "I didn't want to shirk my duty."

I admired his conscientiousness, and inquired, "Would you like a cup of coffee to warm you up?"

"Love one."

"Follow me," I gestured, taking him back to the apartment where he drank two cups. He was reluctant to talk. When he had finished his coffee, I said, "Come on, let's begin the shadowing again."

"Okay," he said, "but please, Lady, don't go through the tail end of changing lights."

I promised that I wouldn't, and drove away, he following me.

Every time I went out driving, he was always behind me. Then I decided to teach Woody a lesson where it would really hurt—the pocketbook. I took my little sister to Santa Barbara—realizing, of course, that Woody would be charged by the mile. The round trip totaled 180 miles, and regardless of how low a price the detective agency might have been charging him, Woody was going to hit the ceiling.

At Santa Barbara we had a cup of coffee at a restaurant, and immediately headed back to Los Angeles. It was the most expensive cup of coffee in the tumultuous life of W.C. Fields.

For three days after he received the agency's report, no one could really call him a comic. He stalked around the house, playing the role of an abused tragedian.

I was beginning to tire of the chase. The next day I drove all over the county, both on crowded and deserted roads. It was difficult for the detective to maintain a constant distance between the two cars, and when he came within vocal range, I'd stick my head out of the window and release sporadic operatic outbursts that sometimes frightened grazing cows. Other times I just rolled down the windows and laughed maniacally with all the volume I could. Once I even got an echo.

Suddenly one day there were two detectives following me, both in the same car. The first one must have wanted to prove to the second that I was off my rocker. I did my best to convince him. My sister and I would go into a restaurant, order food, notice the detectives also ordering something; then, the moment our order appeared, we'd pay the check and leave, heading for another restaurant.

The men would jump up, gaze hungrily at the uneaten food on their plates, and follow us. It was a game that adults play, and they were losing—to say nothing of the man who hired them. We went to pretty popular restaurants, such as Little Joe's or Barney's Beanery, and some of the patrons must have thought the food rather poisonous when they saw four persons walk out at the same time, leaving their plates untouched.

The poor detectives must have been starving. We weren't, because I always saw to it that we carried an ample supply of sandwiches in the car.

Tired of handing out cash and receiving written investigational reports that showed I was leading a chaste life, Woody demanded a meeting with the detectives. I learned afterward that they told him, "The woman is a crazy opera singer."

"I could have told you that before you followed her, and saved five-hundred dollars," Woody retorted.

One of the detectives revealed, "We can't keep up with her."

"And I can't keep up with the expenses," Woody returned, and dismissed their services.

* * * * * * * * * *

Often when Woody's secretary was busy or not working, he had me tend to some of his correspondence. That's when I first suspected that his marriage of years before was still legal. He sent checks for small sums of money to Mrs. Harriet V. Fields, and I learned that he was the father of her son.

He had also sired another son, this one illegitimate, whose mother was a former Ziegfeld Follies beauty. Each week he sent her a check.

I mentioned it to him, and he shrugged it off with, "A night of pleasure can cause a swollen abdomen nine months later."

The mother of the child died, and the youngster was sent to a friend in New York City to be reared.

One day Woody came into my room waving a letter from the woman, in which she said she was going to send the boy out to California to see him as soon as she saved up enough money.

"I have something for you to mail to her," he said.

Certain that he meant money for the boy's trip, I was very happy. Despite his frequent parsimony, I had seen many examples of his generosity, and was sure that this was another magnificent gesture.

He handed me a railroad timetable.

I studied it. It dealt with a railroad running from New York to Florida.

"What good would this do?" I asked. "The boy could never reach Los Angeles if he were put on this train."

"Do as you're told, crafty wench," he ordered.

When he left the room I tossed the timetable into the wastebasket.

A month went by. Woody was exercising in the gymnasium under the watchful eyes of Bob Howard and Sam Hardy when the doorbell rang. I answered it. A bashful boy, the image of Fields, stood outside. Timidly he told me his name, that he was fifteen-years old, and had come from Newark to see his father.

I invited him in, and noticed that he limped. "Is anything wrong with your feet?" I asked him.

"I froze them hitchhiking here," he said.

"You hitchhiked all the way from New York?"

"Only from Albuquerque, New Mexico," he said. "That's as far as my money would take me."

I ran upstairs and broke the news to Woody. He was lifting two iron dumbbells, which he dropped with a crash, barely missing Hardy's toes.

"Repeat that," he requested.

I did.

"Are you ribbing me?" he rasped.

"You know me better than that."

He turned to Hardy. "Get rid of the boy!"

"Just a minute," I interjected. "How can you be so heartless? He's your son."

"Only because nature played a hideous trick on me."

"Won't you even talk with him?" I asked.

"No."

"He's the living image of you, Woody," I said, hoping this disclosure would soften him.

"Then he's a handicapped child."

I tried another approach. "The poor kid has frozen feet."

"Let him warm them on someone else's hearth."

"But they're really frozen," I insisted. "From hitchhiking to see his father."

"A likely story," Woody scoffed. "One to gain sympathy."

"Can he juggle?" Hardy asked me.

I didn't answer.

Hardy said to Woody, "I got a great idea. I can see the billing in lights: W.C. FIELDS AND SON."

Woody made a menacing gesture and Hardy retreated. Then Woody reached into the pocket of a sweat suit he had on, and handed Hardy some money. "Put him on the first train to New York, Sam."

Hardy did as he was bid. Woody never laid eyes on the boy, and neither did I again until years later, after the death of his father.

Angrily I faced Woody and reproached, "You didn't even offer him anything to eat."

He snapped his fingers. "Why, it slipped my mind. I should have offered him a martini."

"A martini for a fifteen-year-old boy?"

"If he's my son, as he says he is, he'd drink it down and ask for another."

"Woody," I said seriously, "you're impossible."

I must say in Woody's defense, that sometimes he was an easy touch for destitute former stage and screen personalities. Many just pocketed the money as if they were entitled to it and didn't even thank him. I remember him paying the electric light bill of one big movie star, plus $500 in back rent.

Once Woody's life was touched by one of the most unforgettable characters that ever lived, an aging Irish woman named Katie Moriarity, from whom Woody purchased fifty one-piece corsets. Should this seem puzzling (and I'm sure that it does) I'll attempt to explain in an orderly fashion.

One day the doorbell rang and the butler summoned me. "There's a strange-looking woman here, Madam," he reported, "who wishes to speak with the woman of the house."

Going downstairs, I found Woody already at the front door engaged in a bizarre conversation. "You remind me of a sergeant I used to know, named Elmer Quizzenberry, who served in World War I," I heard him tell the visitor. "Were you by any chance in that fracas?"

A woman's shrill voice piped up, "I'm in every fracas. I *was* the First World War, sir."

That initial sentence won Woody over to her side. This woman, doughty and red of face, was evidently a fighter, a person who had been buffeted about in the world, but able to battle it out with the best of them.

"Come in," Woody invited.

She entered carrying something resembling a huge sample case, puffing hard from the exertion. Woody gallantly assisted her, set the case down, and said, "My good woman, would it seem presumptuous if I offered you a sampling of the grape?"

"Being my name is Katie Moriarity, I don't think you'd be insulting me," came the answer.

"Irish, I take it," Woody stated.

"Irish," she readily admitted, "but you don't take it anywhere."

Woody introduced us and we sat down at a little table. He poured Mrs. Moriarity about four fingers of straight rye whisky. Before he could ask what she wanted as a mixer or chaser, she drained the glass with a quick backward toss of her head.

"Got a cigar?" she asked her host.

He handed her one. She proceeded to blow out several of the most perfectly oval smoke rings I'd ever seen. I was sorry when they dissipated in the air.

Woody inquired, "What are you selling?"

Opening her large case, Mrs. Moriarity pulled out a one-piece corset. Her eyes strayed to my figure and she shook her head in despair, announcing to Woody, "The lady of the house doesn't need one."

Patting his stomach and purposely expanding it, Woody remarked, "Maybe I do."

"You look to me like you certainly could," snapped Mrs. Moriarity, her eyes trained on Woody's *avoirdupois*.

Woody countered with, "But I only need it for the lower half of my body."

"That's no problem," Mrs. Moriarity said, anxious not to lose a sale, "I'll cut off the top."

Extracting a scissors, she cut away some material and held up the remainder of the garment. Woody began sounding her out on assorted subjects, and pouring more drinks. I could tell he had great esteem for this woman, and sensed she had a trace of larceny in her heart. He soon discovered that she had a great deal more than a trace, as she began a tirade against the Los Angeles Transit Line. Streetcars were her daily target.

It seemed she was opposed to giant companies, often battling them singlehandedly. She lay awake nights planning strategy—small scale as it might be—of how to snip away at their corporate profits. Woody termed this thinking "majestic" because it dovetailed with his own. They enjoyed an instant camaraderie.

In the course of Mrs. Moriarity's loquacity—and two stiff drinks later—we learned how she had ridden on streetcars absolutely free for nearly a month, because, although she had the correct fare in her purse, she would hand the conductor a twenty-dollar bill. In consideration for other passengers boarding the car and not wanting to hold them up or to fall behind the schedule, he would wave Mrs. Moriarity on. However, there was one surly conductor who spoiled her little game. He had been laying for her and had her change already counted out in nickels, dimes and pennies in a small canvas bag. Mrs. Moriarity met her first defeat, but her Waterloo had come after a long string of consecutive victories.

Another trick was to carry an old crumpled transfer and initiate an argument that it was good. She was adept at starting any sort of donnybrook. The fights were always loud and clear and carried the length of the car. Invariably, as Mrs. Moriarity seemed on the verge of losing the controversy, she would suddenly discover the car had reached her destination. She always slowly alighted, and with great dignity; and then, from where she was standing in the street, she would hurl some final barroom invective that scorched the ears of her oppressor.

Another cause for combat came up when the transportation company decided to economize on their public service and eliminate conductors, leaving it up to the motorman to collect the fares. This move was meat for Mrs. Moriarity, who insisted, "There's only one man operating on this car instead of two, and I'm only paying half fare." And half fare was all she paid.

Occasionally she came up with a new gimmick, such as refusing to pay fare on any public conveyance containing no restroom.

Woody talked often with her on the telephone, and her connivings and petty larcenous tactics periodically lifted his spirits. He tried to get her to come to the Paramount lot to harass a director, but Mrs. Moriarity refused.

She lived in a dreary little apartment in the east part of Los Angeles, where we once visited her. The place was spick and span—so clean, in fact, that she discovered the landlord had been showing her apartment to prospective tenants while she was out selling corsets in various parts of the city.

She quickly concocted a scheme to put an end to this invasion of privacy. Procuring a huge brown sack from the market, she carefully placed it on the floor just inside the door, after first having printed upon it in bold crayon: DON'T RENT AN APARTMENT IN THIS BUILDING. THE GODDAMNED PLACE IS FULL OF COCKROACHES.

A few days later, the landlord, angered by her actions after having lost a good prospect, gave her notice to vacate the premises. Wielding a broom, she chased him down the hall.

However, Mrs. Moriarity did move at month's end, but not before she bought from a fish bait store several dozen crickets that according to the proprietor "were in good voice." She managed to squeeze every last one of them under a crack in the landlord's door. She later contacted a neighbor to learn that the man who had evicted her had spent a fortnight of sleeplessness.

Woody never forgot Mrs. Moriarity. He could identify with her. In many ways she was his counterpart, and their activities complemented one another. Fighting as she did against overwhelming odds, a lone but far from defenseless woman, won his undying admiration. The last trick she pulled just before death claimed her was perhaps the one he respected above all others. She went into the produce section of a large market and carried out a basket of partially damaged fruit that was drastically reduced in price. The market manager, in hot pursuit, caught her half a block from the store and accused her of stealing.

She seized him by the coat lapels. "Just a minute, young man," she admonished. "You should be thankful I'm helping you get rid of your garbage without charge."

About those fifty-one corsets Woody bought out of sheer generosity: They were stored in the garage. After Mrs. Moriarity passed away he asked me to take them down to the Los Angeles Harbor. I was to offer them at cut rate to owners of sailboats for patching up their canvas. Naturally I refused.

Another character, but one with whom Woody found he had little in common, was Nick the Greek, cognomenized the world's greatest gambler. They were destined to share one thing, though: Both were to die on Christmas Day, twenty years apart.

I had heard of Nicholas Andrea Dandolos—as who hadn't?— and he had been described to me as a tall, handsome, soft-spoken man of strong ethics whose blood pressure, heart and pulse never varied when he played cards or dice for hundreds of thousands of dollars. Apocryphal stories—that most believed true— mentioned that the man born in Crete had on more than one occasion gambled for eight days and nights without sleep.

He was coming over to the house, and I was looking forward to meeting him, but not as much as Woody was. Up early, he had practiced at the pool table, shuffled and dealt cards, swung a few golf clubs on the lawn, and tried out a new grip on a tennis racket.

"Why this sudden burst of energy?" I asked, curiously.

"Preparation for the arrival of the Greek," he said. "He's a man of action, and I mean to accommodate him." Extracting a quarter from his pocket, he flipped it into the air, called "heads," and caught the falling coin on the back of his hand. Slowly uncovering it, he announced happily, "Heads it is. Nicholas Andrea Dandolos, I am ready."

The butler ushered the gambler into the sitting room. He was immaculately dressed in a powder blue sports coat, gray flannel slacks, white shirt, and blue speckled tie. Handsome to a degree, hair black and wavy, the Greek projected an old-world charm that could descend on a woman unerringly.

After exchanging bits of desultory conversation such as, "How's the weather at Las Vegas?" and Nick answering, "Air conditioned around the crap tables," Woody asked his guest what he would like to drink.

"Nothing, thanks," Nick replied.

"You mean, sir," Woody said incredulously, "that you don't indulge in libations?"

"Occasionally a sip of brandy—nothing more," Nick answered.

The talk veered toward motion pictures, and Woody wanted to know if Nick had seen him in any, and if so, was there anything he particularly enjoyed.

"One episode stands out," the gambler recalled. "You sold a 'talking dog' to a sucker at a carnival. After the sale was consummated, the buyer made some snide remark at which you took umbrage. Then the dog in a hurt voice vowed that he'd never speak again. 'He means it, too,' was your comment as you, the ventriloquist, departed."

Woody laughed. "I guess you admire a slick con man."

"Not at all," Nick declared with passion. "Your little gambit, all done in fun, was the exception. I deplore cheating and deception. If you once get cheated or taken, it can affect your evaluation of all other people. It can arouse a general suspicion and disregard for mankind. Every time you evince disappointment in another person, something within us dies."

Woody gulped and changed the subject. "Do any gambling systems work?"

The Greek shook his head. "Only for a short while. Time and percentages will always part you from your money. I don't even consider the solar system reliable."

Woody inquired, "Care to play a game of pool?"

Nick declined.

The host tried again. "Golf, perhaps?"

Nick shook his head.

"Tennis?"

"I despise most forms of physical exercise," Nick said.

Woody made one more try. "Care to flip coins?"

"I didn't bring any," Nick answered.

After foregoing his effort to lure Nick into some game that gave him an advantage, Woody said, "You will have lunch?"

Nick smiled. "Happy to."

The meeting had certainly been a stalemate. Lunch was about the only common ground. Both ate sparingly. After lunch and a short chat, they shook hands and parted.

I don't know what Nick thought of Woody, but I do know what Woody thought of Nick. "A fine, intelligent gentleman," was his character summation.

"Very wary, too," I concluded.

He concurred.

* * * * * * * * * *

I had guessed that Woody's reputation for hating dogs was invented by some studio publicity department, but I learned that for the most part, he came by it honestly. While I lived with him he owned several dogs. One was a wirehair named Poochie whom he loved to tickle under the chin. She adored him, but was a fickle dog who transferred her affections to Della mainly because the cook fed her. Woody would call to the dog, and the animal started toward him; then, believing she might cadge a handout from Della, she'd turn around and head for the kitchen.

Woody yelled at me, "Get rid of that mangy four-legged beast!"

I asked how.

"By cannon fire, the guillotine, some deep ravine—any way you see fit. I'll leave it to one of your ingenious notions." Then he had a change of heart. "Give Poochie to Della."

So Poochie had a new owner.

For a time Woody seemed quite fond of a Scotch terrier until the day the dog jumped into a friend's lap. Again Woody disowned his dog, and the animal went home with a new master.

A schnauzer named Max was his next love, but Woody had difficulty making the animal obey, and often Max treated his master coolly. "What can you expect," Woody philosophized, "from a descendant of an unromantic nation whose language contains words like 'spitzengefuehl' and 'menschenkenntnis.' "

One beautiful Sunday afternoon, I was riding along the coast highway with Woody near Malibu; the beaches were crowded, the road heavy with traffic.

He began mixing a martini from the car's bar, when Max chose an inauspicious time to show his affection by jumping into the comic's lap, jostling his owner's elbow, and spilling the drink.

"Drat you, lowest of beasts," Woody shouted wrathfully, and picking up the innocent offender, dropped him from the window.

I'm an animal lover, and shouted to the chauffeur, "Stop the car!" I hopped out and rescued the bewildered Max. A hundred horns must have been tooting at me as I exposed my rear end to the northbound traffic while stooping over to pick him up.

* * * * * * * * * *

Why, I'll never know, but Woody hired a gargantuan man with bulging muscles who seemed to be constructed of solid granite instead of flesh and bone. At first I thought he was to be a bodyguard, but learned that he was hired as a butler.

Woody called him—but not to his face—"The Chimp."

Angry because I had not been consulted about his hiring, and believing that it was a mistake, I told Woody, "Yes, 'The Chimp' was hired by 'The Chump.' "

"He can double as a bodyguard," Woody said.

"The only protection you need is from your bad habits," I remarked.

He grinned. "That's not a bad line. I may use it sometime."

"You do, and I'll sue you."

Shaking his head sadly, he intoned, "Et tu, Brutes."

The Chimp converted part of the garage into his private gymnasium, installing heavy weights and suspending enormous rings on ropes for workouts. Day by day he became more belligerent, and there was no question but that Woody was afraid of him. Our new butler was sullen, slow to execute orders, and failed to fit into the unsuspecting role of dupe in any of Woody's Machiavellian schemes.

"He's got to go," Woody declared.

"Then fire him," I advised.

"In time," Woody said. "All in good time. A man such as The Chimp must be canned at a propitious moment."

That propitious moment presented itself within a few days. The Chimp was in the midst of taking some enormous swings on the rings when the rope holding them either broke or unfastened and the giant catapulted through the air, to land on his head and smash a pile of old furniture that was to be donated to the Salvation Army.

The Chimp was out for about five minutes. The second he appeared to have regained consciousness, Woody bent over him and said sternly, "You're fired!" and left the garage.

Staggering to his feet, The Chimp muttered, "I'm going to sue Mr. Fields."

"Why?" I asked.

"Because as I went sailing through the air, I heard someone laugh from that part of the garage," he said, pointing at a dark corner.

"You must be mistaken," I said, frightened.

"There's no mistake."

I related The Chimp's intentions to Woody, who speculated, "I wonder who could have been in the garage at the time of the fortunate disaster." With that, he wrote out a check, adding a bonus to it for The Chimp, who collected his baggage and gymnastic apparatus, and sporting a huge bump on his head, peacefully left the house.

* * * * * * * * * *

Woody was not a connoisseur of art. No treasures hung in any of his houses. He was, however, a collector of paintings done by his good friend and drinking companion, John Decker, and paid as high as $500 for some of the canvases—Decker was always in need of money. John frequently managed to borrow back the pictures, and never returned them. Woody didn't care. Decker amused him, and this was one instance where Woody was willing to pay for his amusement.

The artist did one pen-and-ink drawing that delighted Woody. It depicted Jack Barrymore in a hospital bed, Woody in an adjoining one; both were receiving transfusions from a huge jar of alcohol. To me, the picture hit too close to home. I shuddered every time I looked at it.

When Woody died, he willed this drawing to Dave Chasen, who hung it in his restaurant. He also left him his cane and high hat, as well as two additional Deckers. One of the two remains hidden behind a restaurant couch, too pornographic to display. Woody had it in his house, along with another of equally bad taste. I asked him if he would do me a favor and take them down. Instead, he bought some black yardage and hung it over the pictures.

Woody's coterie of friends often reminisced about their early lives, but he showed little inclination to talk about his true past. He would rave on in hyperbolical nonsense, loving to blacken his own character through exaggeration. Memories of his early struggles were far too painful. I remember when a vaudevillian he once knew, named Jimmy Sargent, approached him on the studio lot and recalled one of Woody's adventures of yesteryear.

"Those were the good old days," Sargent said.

"May they never come again," Woody answered in sepulchral tones.

Often when he was mellow, particularly before bedtime, he talked to me in fatherly fashion, delivering sort of semi-lectures. During one of these, he said, "My little chickadee, I'm going to see to it that you'll be protected, happy, and have financial security the rest of your life."

"Oh, Woody," I said gratefully, "that isn't necessary." In those days I was a happy-go-lucky person, entertaining few serious thoughts of the future, living from day to day. I was sure Woody meant that he wanted to set up some kind of trust fund to provide me with later-in-life protection.

"It *is* necessary," he insisted.

"If you wish, Woody."

"Here is what I am going to give you," he began.

I waited.

"Sound advice," he said. "Don't ever open your mouth first in a business deal. Let someone else do the talking. The person who talks the most has the bigger chance to make a fool of himself first. A fish that opens his mouth gets caught. The fish that keeps it closed swims happily ever after. If I can pound that into your head, your future is assured. You'll have money and be happy."

He gave me an example: "A Paramount producer said he had heard I did a trick pool playing act and would like to use it in a picture. I cogitated a full minute and then told him that I vaguely recalled the skit and would brush up on it. The damned fool offered me several thousand dollars for a few minutes of my artistic tomfoolery. Although considered a genius, he didn't know that I had done the same act frequently. I just picked up my crooked cue, went over to the lot, did an honest hour's work, and took the money."

Woody seldom offered a word to the wise unless invited to give counsel. Unrealistic as it may seem, a grocery delivery boy who frequently brought goods to the house, conferred with Woody—of all experts!—on how to impress his girl friend. He was deeply immersed in love trouble, and on a recent occasion during a quarrel, had been called by the choice of his heart (among other things) "not daring," and "unimaginative."

After pondering the situation, Woody said, "You have to have a device [the word *gimmick* hadn't been coined yet] to startle and make her appreciate you for your originality."

The youth listened attentively, hanging on every word as though it were the Sermon on the Mount.

"Does she work or go to school?" Woody inquired.

"She works in a bank. A teller."

Woody began slowly pacing, hands clasped behind his back, reminding me of an ice skater. "Let me cogitate for a moment, my boy." He seemed lost in deep thought. At length he halted and uttered, "I've got it. Pay close attention to my words of wisdom."

"Yes, Mr. Fields." The boy moved closer to him so as not to lose a single word.

"You print a note in large letters. Very legible. Have it read: THIS IS A STICKUP. I WANT YOUR LIPS. LEAN FORWARD. MAKE NO NOISE. When she complies, you kiss her and walk out without a word."

The youth clapped his hands gleefully. "A wonderful idea!" he exclaimed joyously, and inquired, "Did you ever practice this yourself, Mr. Fields?"

Woody replied, "In a way, but not exactly. A slight re-wording. My note always said: THIS IS A STICKUP! HAND OVER THE MONEY!"

Six months later Woody received a postcard from the youth, postmarked Grand Canyon. "Everything worked out fine, thanks to your suggestion."

Some years later I was reading in the newspaper about a bank stickup. The holdup was thwarted and the bandit caught. It was none other than the same youth.

I accused Woody, "You probably gave him the idea."

"Well, maybe so," he admitted, "but I don't disapprove. I never like to stand in the way of a man bettering himself."

Some important Hollywood personages wouldn't touch Woody with a long pole. In 1939 after Paramount found him too difficult to work with, Arthur Hornblow, Jr., a capable and top producer, said, "I wouldn't have him for five million dollars." Upon hearing of the statement, Woody's comment was, "That makes us only a little over a million apart."

Hornblow's utterance was prompted by Woody's behavior when someone came up with the idea of having him play a trick calliope which had everything fall off—the keys, pipes, etc.— and which finally blew up. It was pure, but expensive slapstick, as the calliope cost thousands of dollars to build, and in those days, it was considered a lot of money for five minutes of laughs.

Eddie Sutherland, the director, asked Woody what he thought of the idea. He wasn't happy. "No," he said. "I can do anything with my hands, but press the keys, no. That's not me. That's for someone like Ed Wynn."

Sutherland conveyed Woody's feelings to the producer. Hornblow said he thought he could win him over. Sutherland didn't think so. Hornblow represented management, and Woody was an enemy of any management. Hornblow coaxed him for three solid days, gave him a sales pitch, and finally asked if he would do it. The answer was "Yes."

But Sutherland thought otherwise. He knew Woody well. "I can almost know what he's thinking by those gimlet eyes," he used to say.

During the shooting Woody sat down before the calliope but refused to play. Not a single note came out. So, from an irritation standpoint, Hornblow had good reason to wash his hands of Fields.

To continue with his business lesson to me, we went to Universal. They were starved for a comic and had made overtures to Woody; and he needed a job badly—not for the money involved, but for the sake of his nerves. Making at least one picture a year seemed to quiet them temporarily.

We sat around a conference table, exchanging pleasantries. The conversation was aimless. There was much lighting of cigarettes and cigars.

One of the executives finally said casually, "What do you want for making us a picture, Bill?"

He nudged me with his elbow as he said, "I'll let you do the talking." He just sat twiddling his fingers and thumbs, smoking his long cigar, looking wise, and listened. The film under discussion was to be produced by Lester Cowan, and directed by George Marshall. Edgar Bergen and his two wooden dummies, Charlie McCarthy and Mortimer Snerd, were to be in the cast which also included Constance Moore.

Conversation died away until a company vice-president said, "We've got to have an inkling of what you want, Bill."

Woody retaliated with, "I'm not going to tell you what I want because I want too much."

One of the blunter executives said, "Having you in a picture is not without certain risks, Mr. Fields. If I may be very frank, let me say that it is bruited about Paramount that you drink all the time."

Woody jumped to his feet and pointed his cane at the executive. "That, sir, is a damned lie!"

The executive backed down by saying, "It's only a rumor."

"Such charges are preposterous, ridiculous, and slanderous," Woody scoffed. "I certainly do not drink all the time. I have to sleep, you know."

The studio head who had thus far been content to sit back and listen, jumped into the fray with an offer of $125,000. It was most generous, far exceeding the expectations of the comic. Woody remained noncommital for a few minutes. Then, deeply

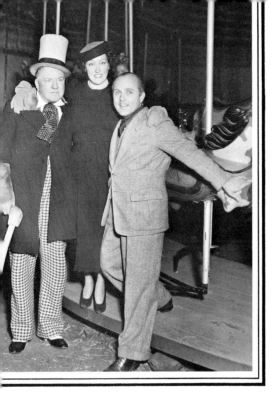

Fields, Gloria Swanson, and
Bobby Vernon on the set of
Poppy (1936), the film version
of Fields' Broadway vehicle
(RAYMOND ROHAUER)

Fields, Don Ameche, Charlie McCarthy and Edgar Bergen on one of their
broadcasts

The Wooden One and The Great One carried their running airtime feud into *You Can't Cheat an Honest Man* (1939) (RAYMOND ROHAUER)

This publicity still notwithstanding, Fields had excellent coordination. He once fell down a flight of stairs without spilling a drop of the martini in his hand (RAYMOND ROHAUER)

Fields' clowning on the golf course was usually intended to give his opponents superfluous confidence ... (RAYMOND ROHAUER)

... And his one-man sandstorms were quite often directed at them (RAYMOND ROHAUER)

This still from *The Barber Shop* sums up "Woody's" feelings about music. He once beat Carlotta with a cane for practicing the guitar (RAYMOND ROHAUER)

Possibly in a mood similar to this one, he remarked to another female vocalist, "You sound like a squeak from a plugged nostril!" (RAYMOND ROHAUER)

The rented mansion "Woody" and Carlotta shared in Bel Air

The house on De Mille Drive—Fields' last home

The entrance to the house on De Mille Drive. "Woody" had it wired with hidden microphones and loudspeakers

Fields recreated his famous pooltable routine for the last time in *Follow the Boys* (1944) (RAYMOND ROHAUER)

John Decker's portrait of "Uncle Willie" as Queen Victoria (WILLIAM MONTIJO)

Fields at the sanitarium with Dr. Ed Hertford, his good friend and admirer. This is the last picture ever taken of "Woody," one week before his death on Christmas Day, 1946 (WILLIAM MONTIJO)

Fields' 1938 sixteen-cylinder Cadillac, which Carlotta inherited and keeps in good running condition

Carlotta Monti as she is today (PHOTO: MAURINE)

sighing a sigh that had anguished overtones, asked, "What about the advance?"

A check was quickly written and handed to him. The amount was $10,000. Woody glanced at it. He tore the check into shreds, tossed the confetti into the air, and stated unequivocally, "You may stick this up your collective asses, gentlemen."

Faces fell, and a long silence developed. Then one of the executives asked, "Did you have any particular price in mind, Mr. Fields, for an advance?"

"Yes, I did," Woody said, blowing a perfect smoke ring into the motionless air. "I want $50,000."

"Impossible!" the studio head said. Evidence of perspiration had gathered on his brow.

"Gentlemen," Fields said sweetly, upon realizing a positive impasse had been reached, "I don't believe you understand. The advance is not just on my acting, but includes the purchase of an original story."

"By whom?" he was asked.

"Charles Bogle."

"One of our writers?" they wanted to know.

"No, a fresh new one. A brilliant meteor streaking across the skies of success."

The studio officials looked at one another, back again at Woody. They were busy men—perhaps they had failed to note the progress of someone new in the writing field. A spokesman said, "We're only faintly familiar with this writer. Do you attest to his abilities?"

"I do, sir. I put my unqualified stamp of approval on him. He is a brainy one. An expert in his line."

Woody was asked, "When can we talk with him?"

"Sir," Woody straightened in his seat and puffed up his chest, until—he confided to me later—"I could hear the olives crashing against each other in my stomach," and went on to say, "*I* am Charles Bogle."

The upshot of it all was that a new check was issued to Fields for $50,000, and he received screen credit for the original story of *You Can't Cheat an Honest Man,* much of which he improvised when it came time to play the scenes. In the film he was Larson E. Whipsnade, a circus impresario.

He was to star in three more successive pictures for Universal: *My Little Chickadee* with Mae West, *The Bank Dick,* and *Never Give a Sucker an Even Break,* followed by a guest role in *Follow the Boys.*

Before he finished with Universal, a studio bigwig recalled the remark of Arthur Hornblow, Jr., and said of the Paramount official, "His price was too cheap when he said he wouldn't do another picture with Fields for five million dollars. Our price would be double that."

On the way home after the initial deal with Universal, Woody was in a gay mood, punctuated with much laughing and drinking. Tears of pure joy were running down his craggy cheeks. He was happiest if he got the best of someone in a money deal, even if the amount were trifling, and he felt that this just concluded contract was one of his greatest pecuniary triumphs.

"I'd have accepted $50,000 for doing the entire picture," he acknowledged. "And remember, Chinaman," he said to conclude the lesson, "business is an establishment that gives you the legal, even though unethical, right to screw the naïve —right, left, and in the middle."

I recall the time La Cava asked, "Why don't you ever give a sucker, or anyone else for that matter, an even break? Why must you always gouge him down to the last penny? Why do you have to always put the squeeze on him?"

"I will explain the reasons behind my philosophy," Woody said solemnly. "Most people have a feeling they are going to be reincarnated and come back to this life. Not me. I know I'm going through here only once."

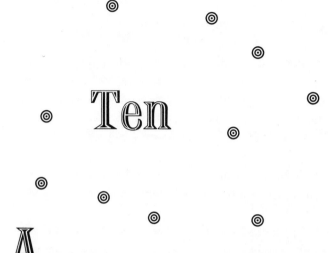

Ten

ALTHOUGH Woody had practically muted my singing voice, music was so permanently in my heart that I had to have an outlet. Periodically I sang at the El Paseo and the El Cortijo (which rhymes with Montijo) in Santa Barbara, on radio, and in a San Diego nightclub. He didn't mind this too much, as I was close to home. And upon my return I was always in a wonderful mood, due to the lift in spirits I got from being in the entertainment spotlight again.

Even though I had gotten some of the singing out of my system, I still needed to express myself, so I bought a Spanish guitar. After the first lesson I came home to practice. All I learned was one chord, and it went "Vrummm . . . vrummm . . . vrummm."

Woody stood over me while I strummed the instrument. "Chinaman," he said, "that's wonderful . . . really wonderful. I want you to play that at my funeral."

Although aware of his dislike for music, I thought he really meant it, and I kept playing the single chord over and over again. The next thing I knew, he jerked me out of the chair and was whacking my backside with the cane he used in comedies, to his own vocal cadence of "Vrummm . . . vrummm . . . vrummm."

Screaming with pain, I ran to my room and telephoned the police. When they arrived, one of them called it "a lover's spat," and predicted it would soon pass over. I didn't think so. My Spanish blood was boiling. I packed two large suitcases, jammed on my head a screwy hat made from two silver foxes with which he'd gifted me, and called to him, "I'm going to New York and you'll never see me again. I can sing and play there to my heart's content."

"And the buildings will quiver and crumble and fall into the sea, and the island of Manhattan will forever sink from sight," he droned.

I left, but in my haste I had forgotten my guitar. Sure that the instrument had met a cruel death at his hands, I bought myself another in New York.

After only a few days in Manhattan, I had a stroke of good fortune in landing a job at the White Hotel. I sang Spanish songs and did impersonations which included Garbo, Hepburn, and Dietrich. Expanding my mimicking repertoire, I included W.C. Fields. Afterward, mingling with the patrons, I heard a woman comment: "You'd almost have to live with Fields to do so realistic an impersonation as Miss Monti did."

Hardly a day passed that I didn't hear from Woody either by letter, telegram, or telephone. Still distrustful of women, he was afraid to put any tenderness into writing, but periodically an "I miss you" crept into the correspondence—which coming from him, was comparable to a mad declaration of eternal love.

His lengthier letters all had the distinct Fieldsian touch. Here is one that I saved:

Dear dear Chinaman:

Nothing of interest to write. Yesterday morning we had a fire which destroyed part of the house, but I'm not worried because my five insurance policies will see me through, although I expect some strong arguments from the white collar men who sold them to me. They can always smell arson a mile away. Perhaps closer. Did you ever notice all insurance men are lookalikes?

The weather has been marvelous, and you could have sat by the pool and added a tan to your already beautiful tan. Two coats, according to Wilfred Smirch, my painter, are better than one. Please remember the California climate as you walk down those cold streets, with the Atlantic breezes whistling up anything of yours they can get into.

A drama critic wrote yesterday that 'W.C. Fields had a princely air about him.' I'd much sooner have a prince's income and a foul air about me.

When you come back to me we can play duets. You on your (ugh!) guitar, accompanied by me swinging a cat by the tail with one hand and tweaking my nose with the other.

My bunion—the reliable one you sometimes step on—predicts that the typhoon season will be horrendous this year. I want you here before it begins. I will batten up all your hatches and you will survive it quite comfortably.

> With regards,
> Oscar Treadmill

P.S. By the way, do you remember Winston, my pet water buffalo? After you left I moved the beast into your suite so he could have more comfortable quarters. Yesterday he broke loose and escaped to the city streets where he was given a traffic ticket for jaywalking and failure to extend his right horn on a turn. Oh well, such is humdrum life in the Hollywood veldt.

During my singing engagement I met and became infatuated with a Broadway stage singer who was beginning to establish a national reputation. He was conceited, arrogant, and demanding

—but what a voice! It had enormous range and beautiful tonal qualities. I believe that was what I fell in love with. He asked me to marry him. A girl on the rebound can say yes in a hurry to a matrimonial proposal, and such was my answer.

I wrote Woody and broke the news. It was a difficult letter to write, and my tears smeared some of the ink.

His reply was a serious one. "I only hope you are marrying the right fellow, as you need special handling. I'm going to give you twenty-five dollars per week as a continuous wedding present. Pick it up at the National City Bank. At least I'll feel better if I know you'll have coffee and doughnuts."

Now he disliked singers more than ever—and, this time he had a valid reason.

I telephoned Frank Orsatti, the Hollywood agent, and arranged for a screen test for my new man. Later he was to make two movies.

He had a birthday coming up, and I gave a successful surprise party for him. Among the guests were Walter Huston—his best friend; Maxwell Anderson; and Mike Todd, who said I was the most beautiful girl he had ever seen. I thanked him.

Mike went on, "You know, Bill Fields told me you were prettier than any girl I ever used in any production, but I never believed it. I do now."

"He told you that?" I asked. And then I changed the subject. It was hardly the time to reminisce over Woody.

But the damage had been done.

My fiancé was prevailed upon to sing (he really needed little urging; just the faintest suggestion would have started him off), and he obliged with two numbers. All through them I imagined I heard that familiar grating voice complaining, "Shut off that goddamned sound box and save my eardrums."

Woody was still telephoning me every night, insisting that I also phone him daily, collect. He sounded depressed and kept asking, "Is he the right man for a Chinaman?" adding, "You've got to be careful of these mixed marriages, you know."

I told him that I was positive—but at the same time my mind was vacillating between the East and West coasts and the two men who held my affection.

Meanwhile, as the days and nights of courtship continued with no official marriage date having been set as yet, my intended and I met every evening and spent each weekend together. We hobnobbed with Metropolitan Opera Company performers and had a gay time.

One Saturday morning he telephoned: His fan mail was piling high, and he thought it best to stay home and answer it, but would call me that evening.

Although it was a rather lame excuse, I didn't question it. Should interrogations ever become necessary, I would have plenty of time for them after our marriage. I told him to go ahead and get rid of his obligations, and that I would see him later.

I turned on my radio, but then switched it off again and listened to the rain beating against the windowpanes. Rain in New York can make a person feel lonely and depressed. I was getting bluer by the minute, and decided that the only way to rid myself of these feelings was to go visit my singer . . . just putting my arms around him or holding his hand would elevate my spirits. Forgetting to telephone first, I hopped into a cab. Just as I was about to knock at the door of his apartment, I heard a woman's voice inside.

I stood at the door listening, rooted to the spot. I'm not a chronic eavesdropper, but this time I justified my actions by believing I had the privilege of being one. Certain sounds began filtering through the door that could be unmistakably associated with some sizzling lovemaking. This was more than I could take. I began pounding on the door, and I heard her gasp, "Who could it be?"

"It's Carlotta Monti," I told her.

"My God!" I heard her exclaim. "She'll kill me."

"I might just do that."

My singer—who was already my erstwhile singer as far as I was concerned—came to the door, but refused to open it. He begged me to leave, saying that he would telephone. I told him I was going and not to dare call me—*ever*—and that we were positively through.

I had instantly recognized the other voice—it belonging to a Broadway musical comedy star, a woman who was later to become a film great—and eventually, a suicide. She induced every man she went with to leave his wife and she thereby enjoyed the ultimate in successful love affairs, until a big movie mogul turned her down. The blow to her ego proved fatal. She slipped into a gorgeous nightgown, changed the sheets on her bed, fixed her hair and makeup—and then slashed her wrists. Newspaper photographers had a field day.

I returned to my room more dejected than before I left.

The ringing of the telephone broke into my mood.

It was Woody calling. He said that he was very sick, and he reminded, "Remember the pact you made with me?"

I remembered. It was that as long as he was alive, if he ever needed me, no matter where I was or what I was doing, I would come back to him—and he always added, "even if you're west of the Lesser Antilles." For some reason unknown to me, mention of the Antilles touched a funny bone deep inside him.

I promised I would come back, and before we hung up he asked, "Did you buy another guitar?"

I told him I had.

"Leave it behind," he urged, "and your voice with it."

I promised, and thus ended an Eastern musical career that was just getting off the ground.

* * * * * * * * * *

Los Angeles never looked so good, and poor Woody never looked worse. The ravages of alcohol were beginning to make themselves felt. I heard him ask Eddie Sutherland if Eddie got pleasure from drinking. Eddie answered in the affirmative, and said, "Don't you, Bill?"

"No," Woody returned sadly. "It's medicine for me now."

Together with his secretary, I took him down to Soboba, a hot springs resort where he loved the mineral waters and mud baths. We called in a doctor from a nearby town who attended him daily for about three weeks, usually giving him an injection.

When the bill came, Woody found that the doctor had charged him $1,000 per visit. He was so boiling mad that he temporarily recovered most of his strength—at least enough to call the doctor a "blood-sucking pirate." He went to court and settled for $10,000.

One day at his Soboba Indian-style cottage, Woody was dozing on the porch after dinner. His food intake had consisted of three medium-sized bites of a veal cutlet. "Made me drowsy," he said, "seeing all that food on my plate."

Suddenly he heard footsteps and sat erect—it was the sound of running along a dirt pathway, and up to the porch came two solidly-built young men clad in trunks, sweat shirts, and tennis shoes. When they saw him, they stopped and greeted, "Good evening, Mr. Fields."

Woody took one look at them, and ran inside the cottage, located his pistol, and reappeared on the porch with it in hand. Pointing the long-barreled gun at the two men, he croaked, "Kidnappers, eh?"

At this point I came out, but he pushed me aside. "Women and gunplay don't mix," he said, and ordered, "Go inside and bake a cake."

I refused to budge. The two young men were truly bewildered. One of them explained, "We're fighters, training up here, Mr. Fields, and both of us are admirers of yours."

"Not kidnappers, then?" Woody thought it over.

One of the fighters, glancing at me, said to Woody, "Sir, I don't want to disappoint you, but if we were kidnappers, we'd take this young lady first."

"If you do," Woody replied, "don't bother me with a

ransom note. Address it to any group of singers: They might scrape up some money. But don't send it to any music critics or it will be ignored."

The two fighters moved cautiously toward the porch. After a short interrogation period, Woody was apparently satisfied that the pair were what they claimed to be, and invited them to sit down. They accepted the invitation, and we chatted for about an hour. Woody seemed to enjoy them. Nevertheless, he held the pistol on his lap the entire time.

* * * * * * * * * *

Paramount was interested in Fields for the film version of *Poppy*, the Broadway show he had starred in. Wondering about his physical condition and whether his health could hold up long enough to complete the picture, the studio dispatched Bill LeBaron and Eddie Sutherland to Soboba to make a report. They were to snoop around, analyze his stamina and bring their findings back to the studio.

Woody looked ghastly when they arrived. But a moment later, sensing why they had come, he sprang to his feet, did a monologue, then a pantomime with his hat and cane, and finished by doing a dance.

"I'm my old self, boys," he averred.

The visitors weren't so sure. However, they were certain of one thing: He had guts. On the way back to Los Angeles they discussed his condition, asking each other, "Can he work in a picture?" They both loved him and hated to rule him out due to a diagnosis of poor health.

"How can we sit in judgment on him?" Sutherland finally asked.

LeBaron shook his head. "I don't know. He moved around spryly enough, but maybe he collapsed the minute we left."

"Let's leave it up to a doctor," Sutherland suggested.

"Yes," LeBaron agreed, "the studio insurance doctor."

Before we returned to Los Angeles, we met Dave Chasen; his daughter's father-in-law, Ben Smith; and Gene Fowler.

Smith was known as "Sell 'em short Smith," a man who had made a hundred million dollars in the 1929 stock market crash. He had borrowed stocks, sold them, and then bought them back at a fraction of their sales price.

We went to the Agua Caliente Racetrack, adjacent to Tijuana (it was called Tia Juana, or plain old "Aunt Joanna," in those days), where Chasen owned the food and drink concessions. To avoid the delay of having waiters run up and down the stairs for separate drink orders while the men watched the races, the drinks were brought all at one time. Woody had five martinis lined up before him, Fowler five rums, Smith five small bottles of milk.

A reporter from a San Diego newspaper dropped into a vacant seat at our table. Noticing the milk, he asked, "When did *you* have milk last, Mr. Fields?"

"Just before my mother died," Woody answered.

Both LeBaron and Sutherland knew the type of examination the insurance doctor gave to cast members of a picture. He would ask an actor to open his mouth and say "Ah;" listen to the heart and lungs for a few seconds with a stethoscope; and say, "Goodbye, you're in good health."

As luck would have it, when Woody reported for his examination the regular doctor was on vacation, and substituting for him was an ambitious youth with the ink still wet on his medical diploma.

"I don't know whether or not you know it," he said to Woody, "but at one time you had tuberculosis in both lungs, very badly."

"I guess that goddamned Dutchman was right," Woody exclaimed.

He was referring to a doctor in Berlin who, thirty years before, had told him he'd have to give up his career and drinking and smoking because he had tuberculosis in both lungs.

Somehow Sutherland and LeBaron talked the doctor into passing him, and Woody returned to Soboba to rest up.

But before they started shooting, another doctor ordered him into a hospital in Riverside, because as the doctor said, "This man is dying." He was placed in an oxygen tent and had nurses around the clock. A week later he was discharged, and was back on the Paramount lot playing the role of Professor Eustace McGargle.

Eddie Sutherland was one director who could coax a good performance out of Fields. He knew there was an inconsistency to Woody's performances, and he realized that many times it was due to poor health. "When Bill's good, he's very good, but when he's bad, he's awful," he used to say.

From the beginning of shooting time until quitting time, Fields and Sutherland were bitter antagonists. If some of the guns they used in the pictures had been loaded with real bullets, I think they'd have killed one another.

Woody didn't give a hoot about the story line in a picture —all he wanted was a vehicle for himself. He loved any theme concerning a dirty old man, an ugly woman, and a mean little child. Sutherland loved a well-kempt man, pretty woman, and nice children. This was the crux of many of their clashes. But after the day's shooting was over they were the firmest of friends . . . taking a few drinks, joking together.

One of his wordiest tiffs with Sutherland occurred when Woody wanted to shoot down a kite with a cap pistol. It was an inexpensive sequence to make, but Director Sutherland didn't think it had a place in the picture. As usual, he allowed Fields his wish; but it later died on the cutting room floor.

I once asked Eddie a point blank question: "Why isn't Woody the greatest star in the world?"

Sutherland had a ready answer. "Because women don't like him."

I think he was right.

* * * * * * * * * *

While making *Poppy* for Paramount in 1936, Woody's sacroiliac gave him trouble. He was unable to sit in a regular chair, so studio carpenters constructed a special contraption, an inclined board with arms, on which he rested between scenes. On the studio lot he slept from twelve until two o'clock every afternoon. Strict orders were left that no one was to disturb him.

Across the street from Paramount was a popular restaurant named Lucy's, a favorite lunch spot for the executives, the stars, and anyone else who could afford it. At one noonday meal that Woody had there with LeBaron, the producer was in a hurry and excused himself immediately upon finishing his lunch. Woody, sitting alone, discovered he was too tired and weak to walk the one block back to the studio. Deciding to thumb a ride, he stood on crowded Melrose Avenue, extended his thumb for fifteen minutes, and then gave up. No one recognized him in a tan polo coat and matching cap. He walked slowly back, cursing all the way to his dressing room.

Woody didn't drive too many women to distraction, but among those he did were the script girls—through his ad libbing. The script for one scene in *Poppy* called for him to say, "I will now play the 'Moonlight Sonata.' " It was a simple line, but, instead of delivering it, he mumbled, "I will now render the allegro movement from the Duggi Jig Schreckensnack opera of Gilka Kimmel, an opus Piptitone."

The script girl gasped, and asked how to spell the words. Sutherland wanted an interpretation. Woody shrugged, and admitted, "I don't know myself what it means. To tell you the truth, it just popped out. But leave it in, Eddie, it's got a nice lilt to it."

Eddie left it in.

Another time the script read, "What a lovely cottage." It was a rather innocuous line, before he changed it to "What a charming little lean-to. Reminds me of my wickiup on the Limb-poo-poo."

During the making of *Poppy*, Woody seemed to lose his sense of balance. Many thought he was drunk when he fell down, but he had temporarily lost his equilibrium. Sutherland lined up a number of men alongside of any stretch Woody was required to walk, to catch him when he fell. He was a sick man with the courage of a lion.

Miraculously, he recovered—to the extent that he took a ballet dancer, who had been telephoning the house, with him to Chasen's in company with Bob Howard and his wife. I called a friend at Chasen's to verify my suspicions. Earlier in the week I had accused Woody of seeing her. He turned an aggrieved face toward me and said, "Why, I'd just as soon stick a fork in my mother's back, my little love turtle."

I'll fix him, I thought, but how? At last I hit upon a plan. I telephoned an ambulance company to send one of their cars over to the house. When they arrived I hatched a little plot with the two attendants after bribing them with some cash.

On the evening in question they drove to Chasen's, pulled up in front of that fashionable restaurant, got out—white coats and all—went inside and asked the maitre d', "Where is Mr. Fields?"

The somewhat startled employee pointed to a secluded booth. "Over in the corner."

The white-uniformed men approached the diners. "Mr. Fields?" one of them questioned.

Woody was about to lift his martini glass. He looked at the men in white, back at the martini again, and mumbled, "It's too early in the evening for the D.T.s. I wonder what kind of vermouth Dave's using." He faced the ambulance men. "I am Mr. Fields," he said in a dignified voice, "and may I inquire why you knaves in ice cream suits are interrupting our dinner?"

One of them said, "It was reported that you had a heart attack and we came to pick you up. We're on official business. Please don't be difficult."

"Heart attack?" Woody repeated. "My heart's in perfect condition." To prove it, he thumped it with his fist and began to cough violently. "Ooops," he said, "I must have hit the wrong side."

"Better go with them," Bob Howard advised. "Straighten out the mistake and we'll wait here for you."

Woody left under protest. On the way out of the crowded restaurant a friend saw him and called, "Anything wrong, Bill?"

"No, nothing, my good man," he replied, and to explain the presence of the white-suited attendants who were the focus of all eyes, said, "These gentlemen are from the barber shop. They came to remind me of my appointment."

The patient was delivered to me. I gave him a bawling out and he swore his fidelity.

Eleven

HEN Woody first went on Edgar Bergen's *Chase and Sanborn Hour* radio show (when that medium was booming), the noted ventriloquist admitted he had some trepidation over the comedian's drinking. These fears were soon allayed. "True," Bergen recalled, "he had a shaker of martinis with him most of the time, but I never saw him intoxicated, and to my knowledge, no one ever did."

Before Woody and Bergen had ever met, the ventriloquist received a wire out of the blue which read: FINE COMEDY AND FINE TIMING. YOU ARE A BRIGHT HOPE AND I WOULDN'T MISS ANY OF YOUR SHOWS.

BILL FIELDS

Bergen admits without hesitation that Woody was the greatest guest performer he ever had on his show—and he had them all. "He could not only write comedy," Bergen remembers, "but could deliver in a unique style what was written for him. He could also do pantomime. He was really the last of the triple-threat comedians."

The radio scripts were prepared by two of Hollywood's top comedy writers, Zeno Klinker and Dick Mack. (Mr. Klinker, a gifted speaker, now appears before many clubs and organizations with a program of humorous films of early airplanes and their inventors.)

Here are excerpts:

Charlie: Oh, Mr. Goodwin and Mr. Noble . . .

Goodwin & Noble: What is it, Charlie?

Charlie: We're pals, aren't we, fellows? I can count on you, can't I?

Goodwin: How much do you need?

Charlie: I want nothing but your friendship.

Goodwin: There's more to this friendship than meets the eye. What's the catch, Edgar?

Bergen: Well, you know, our guest, W.C. Fields, and Charlie have often had a difference of opinion.

Noble: So that's it.

Charlie: Are you fellows on my side?

Noble: Of course we are, old boy. If Mr. Fields so much as breaks your leg, I shall write him a nasty letter.

Charlie: Yeah? Thanks for nothing. He better not start anything with me.

Bergen: Quiet, Charlie, here he comes.
(Fields enters singing "Give me my books and my bottle" . . . yodel)

Charlie: Oh, oh, he's coming in on a wing and a snootful.

Fields: Hello, Edgar.

Bergen: Hello, Bill.

Fields: It's good to see you again, Edgar. I must say you're looking in the pink . . . and where is that lovable little nipper, Master Charles McCarthy?

Charlie: Here I am, Mr. Fields . . . right under your nose.

Fields: Right under my nose? (Laughs) I'll ignore that, Charles, because tonight I'm imbued with the spirit of friendship.

Charlie: You're really loaded, eh?

Bergen: It's good to see you, Bill. "Two things improve with age . . . old friends and old wine . . ."

Fields: Don't mind if I do . . . I feel poetic tonight. "Fair grow the lilies on the river bank . . ."

Bergen: Ah, yes. Beside the crystal clear water . . .

Fields: Yes, water. How it nauseates me. I'm allergic to water . . . my grandmother drowned in the filthy stuff.

Charlie: Mr. Fields, what's that you're carrying under your arm?

Fields: Under my arm? . . . Let me see . . . Oh, yes, it's a saw, Charlie. (drops saw)

Charlie: Oh, oh . . . now it starts . . . he's packin' a saw.

Bergen: No, Charlie. Bill, why are you carrying a saw?

Fields: Oh, I was just sawing the grass in my yard . . . it's rather long. I was in a hurry to get here, and I didn't have time to drop the saw.

Charlie: Poppy-cock and piffle-poffle.

Fields: Poppy-cock and piffle-poffle . . . fine language. It just so happens I have been taking a postgraduate course in tree surgery . . . I spent two years as an intern in the petrified forest.

Bergen: Then a saw is an essential part of your equipment?

Fields: Yes, Edgar . . . one never knows when one might run into a little kindling wood . . . or a woodchuck.

Charlie: Is it true, Mr. Fields, that when you stood on the corner of Hollywood and Vine, forty-three cars waited for your nose to change to green?

Fields: Go away, you woodpecker's blueplate, before I take my saw and pedicure your tootsies.

*   *   *   *   *   *   *   *   *   *

Charlie: Did we have to get out here so early, Bergen? It's awful cold. I bet you anything Mr. Fields doesn't even show up.

Bergen: Well, he promised to be here at six-thirty.

Fields:	(Fading in—singing) "Give me my books and my bottle . . ." Oley-o-Oley-o.
Charlie:	Here comes W.C. What an ad for black coffee. Hello, Mr. Fields.
Fields:	Hello, my little chum. I was thinking of you only yesterday.
Charlie:	You were.
Fields:	Yes—I was cleaning out the woodshed at the time.
Charlie:	Yes . . . Mr. Fields, is that your nose or a new kind of flame thrower?
Fields:	Very funny, Charles. What's this kid doing around here, anyway?
Charlie:	I'm going to be your caddy, Mr. Fields, and keep score.
Fields:	Oh-oh!
Bergen:	Well, would you rather I kept score, Bill?
Fields:	Well, to be perfectly frank, I've never trusted either of you.
Charlie:	What do you mean? Bergen is just as honest as you are . . . you crook, you.
Fields:	You better get out of the sun, Charles, before you come unglued.
Charlie:	Do you mind if I stand in the shade of your nose?
Bergen:	Let's not start that, I'm sure Charlie will be a fair scorekeeper.
Fields:	Tell me, Charles, if I take three drives and three putts, what's my score?
Charlie:	Three and three? . . . Four.
Fields:	Very good, very good, Charles. How do you arrive at four?
Charlie:	Well, you see, when you were putting, a quarter fell out of your pocket.
Fields:	Oh, yes, yes . . . Well, that sounds like a workable arrangement.

Bergen:	Isn't it a lovely day, Bill? The air is so intoxicating.
Fields:	Is it? Stand back and let me take a deep breath.
Bergen:	Now quiet, Charlie. Mr. Fields is going to tee off.
Fields:	Yes, quiet, please . . . I shall now take my usual stance.
Charlie:	I wouldn't if I were you . . . the ground is too wet.
Fields:	Quiet, you termite's flophouse.
Bergen:	Charlie, keep quiet. He's getting ready to drive. If you don't mind a suggestion, Bill, you're not holding your club right. Bend your elbow a little more.
Charlie:	Pssh. Telling Fields how to bend his elbow. That's like carrying coals to Newcastle.
Fields:	Charles, my little pal?
Charlie:	Yes, Mr. Fields?
Fields:	Do you know the meaning of rigor mortis?
Charlie:	No sir.
Fields:	Well, you will in a minute.
Bergen:	Now, Bill, let's not start that. Charlie, stop it . . . you have Mr. Fields all unstrung.
Fields:	Somebody get me a sedative . . . with an olive in it.

Woody and Charlie McCarthy had some hilarious running battles. It was a constant feud. Woody was not about to be bested by any wooden dummy, and Bergen tried to keep an even battle going on between them. On the air, each one would slip in a few surprises, departing from the script for some feuding and sneak punches with ad libs. But it was a clean fight flavored with sportsmanship.

There were some jokes in the show that I never forgot. One was when Woody said, "After three days I took a turn for the nurse."

Then another time, Bergen asked, "What are you suffering from, Mr. Fields?"

"Well, I am suffering from Ralfadaldo, complicated by a stubborn case of dandruff."

Lastly: "Mr. Fields, what would your father have said if he knew you drank two quarts of whiskey a day?"

"He would have called me a sissy."

* * * * * * * * * *

Once again Woody said, "Let's move. This house is stifling me." I agreed that it was a good idea and thought perhaps a change of environment would prove a boon to his health. And strangely enough, it did—at least for a number of years.

But before we found another place to live, our three acres of grounds in Bel Air were threatened by a fast-spreading fire. Throughout the years there have been some pretty costly conflagrations in this wealthy residential area, but only the newspapers and victims of the disasters seemed to be concerned. The general public couldn't have cared less if the tenants or the insurance company were the losers. When tragedy strikes the rich, it seems to give the poor a lift.

Woody didn't care either, being unconcerned when we first smelled smoke and saw the red glare in the sky as the hills were ablaze behind the house; but as the blaze drew nearer he was upset by the thought that some of his liquor might be consumed or ruined by fire and smoke.

Only Woody and I and his secretary were there in the twenty-room mansion, as the servants had been given the night off.

We dashed outside. Woody started shouting, "Save the liquor! Save the liquor!" and began prodding me with his cane and exhorting me and his secretary to run into the house and cart out his precious bottles.

"But what about my *clothes?*" I demanded.

"You'll look better without them," he replied. Again he poked his cane into me—this time it hit my thigh. It hurt. "Go get my liquor!"

"I'll be risking my life," I told him.

"You've been doing that every day since you moved in with me," was his answer.

"The firemen ought to be here soon," I said. "They'll save your precious liquor."

"They sure will," he said. "For themselves."

The wind changed, and the flames swept off in another direction. A few minutes more and they would have entered our grounds. All he said was, "I just wanted to see how you girls would act in an emergency."

"How did we?" I asked.

"Froze. You froze in your tracks. You'd both better do something about your reflexes."

He rented a huge house and estate at 2015 De Mille Drive, just across the road from Cecil B. De Mille, in whose honor the street was named. It was in a private park on a rise of ground situated between two busy thoroughfares, Franklin Avenue and "The Boulevard of the Happy Ones"—Los Feliz Boulevard.

In those days Laughlin Park had a faintly aristocratic air, something it has since lost to a large extent. The architecture of houses in the park varied from Mediterranean to Spanish to contemporary American. The roads were narrow, the cars traversing them usually large. Fields wasn't the only celebrity besides De Mille living in Laughlin Park, whose streets lay behind unlatched gateposts. Other dwellers, or former ones, included Antonio Moreno, Jack Dempsey, Anthony Quinn, and Deanna Durbin.

But neither the City of Los Angeles—and Laughlin Park was only a short distance from Hollywood—nor the County paid for the upkeep of the streets. This responsibility continues to fall on the shoulders of the house owners, which presently accounts for a sprinkling of potholes and unswept leaves.

Today this section is still a private park, quiet and semitropical, housing a heterogeneous group ranging from a Superior Court judge to the proprietor of a fresh fish store.

The park dwellers often squabble like small-town neighbors. Taxes and mortgage rates have risen, and some of the older residents are battling to hold onto the houses their families have lived in for many years.

On our first day there I saw Woody inspecting his rifle. When I asked him his intentions, he pointed out the close proximity of Griffith Park and the zoo.

"Why, you can't tell when a hairy-nosed wombat might escape and wander over here to endanger all of us," was his excuse.

The rooms in this new house were more spacious than those of Woody's two previous houses. One was ideal for his pool and Ping-Pong tables; another for an office; and upstairs was perfect for his gymnasium. A handsome chandelier hung over the pool table, and as he always said, "The lighting must be good in this most important room in the house."

Downstairs was his barber shop. He seldom had a barber come to the house, as it was too expensive. His main reason for having the chair was for dozing purposes; he slept better in it than he did in a bed.

It was in the gymnasium that Bob Howard took charge of him. He was majordomo over Woody, and there were no arguments when it came to his physical welfare. Howard had conditioned such celebrities as Myrna Loy, Betty Grable, Irving Berlin, Jon Hall, Cole Porter, Harry Richman, and Lady Mendl.

"I'll improve your figure in two weeks," Howard told Woody.

"Well, just so it doesn't look like Lady Mendl's," was the return comment.

Howard would arrive promptly at two-thirty, five afternoons each week, and wage a steady battle for one- and one-half hours in the gymnasium and on the grounds. Bob was faced with an almost hopeless task: taking weight off Woody and preventing him from sneaking drinks from secret hiding places—one bottle was buried in the midst of the rose garden. For an additional joust, they contested each other in semantics, and I was usually caught and annihilated in a crossfire of over-developed vocabularies.

One cute trick the trainer pulled was to seat Woody on a stationary bicycle facing a bar well stocked with potables, and with the sight of the bottles as an incentive, Woody would pedal fast and furiously.

After a stiff workout he used to thump his chest, flex his muscles, and declare, "I'll fight anyone in pediatrics." To continue his physical education program, he slept with windows wide open on cold nights, a fresh air fiend if I ever saw one. "The incoming ozone charges my drinks with the elixir of life," he told me.

On the set a producer asked him, "Are you keeping fit, Bill?"

"Most assuredly, sir," he replied. "I do three laps around my lake every day."

"Keep up the good work," the producer said.

It was all I could do to keep from laughing out loud. The lake Woody referred to was a goldfish pond whose dimensions were about twenty by eight feet.

For years Bob Howard had tried to attend to Woody's physical education program, and during that time he invented a steam cabinet heated by the rays of the sun. Woody was friendly with Bob's shapely wife, Neel, and at Woody's insistence, she would drop in at the house for a steam bath herself.

Even on foggy days Woody almost demanded that Neel try the cabinet. She began to get suspicious. While she was inside the reducing machine, Woody kept circling it, always stopping in a certain place and staring toward her. All but her head was covered by the cabinet, but she noticed that Woody never seemed to be looking at her face when they conversed. Finally she discovered why: There was a peephole in the canvas. Her baths came to a sudden end.

The Howards had two children, Richard and Bill. Despite

his reputation for loathing pre-pubescents, Woody displayed much affection for the Howard youngsters. Dick was a handicapped child, afflicted with spastic paralysis on one side. Woody chose not to remember this, and brought the boy baseball outfits, bowling equipment—everything wonderful for a healthy youngster to enjoy. He simply bought Dick anything that came into his head. And, of course, the boy was thrilled with the gifts, even though he couldn't use them. I wondered if perhaps Woody thought these presents might create such a longing and desire that Dick would eventually overcome his handicap.

Neel noticed that money always seemed to be jingling in Dick's pockets. She was puzzled. At six he was too young to be a wage earner. She followed him down the street and saw the boy, in the style of a philanthropist, handing out coins and even bills to other children. A confession seemed in order, and she obtained one—the child led her to the basement where a coffee can was hidden. Neel estimated there might have been as much as fifty dollars in it.

Woody, of course, was the culprit.

Bob put Woody on various diets, protein, fruits, and vegetables. Potatoes were taboo. But still he continued to gain weight—it was the liquor. Woody came out of the steam cabinet looking like a rosy cherub. Naturally it was a false innocence, but very deceptive. Then he would be ready for cocktail time.

Bob made Fields jog around the grounds. Woody would wear either shorts or white duck pants. The day he trusted Woody to jog alone, Bob said, "Don't come back into the house until you're soaking wet with perspiration." Woody agreed. The second he was out of sight he picked up a pitcher of martinis and poured it over his body, and returned to the house puffing.

Sniffing him, Bob said he gave up: Woody should be constantly under a doctor's care and never out of his sight. "That's the only way you'll lick your problem," he concluded.

Woody agreed to this suggestion. After a lengthy bargaining

session over prices, he engaged a young doctor Bob recommended. The first step was for the doctor to give Woody a complete physical. The diagnosis (and prognosis) was: "Mr. Fields, if you don't stop drinking you'll be dead in six months."

"Why, that's exactly what a German medico in Baden-Baden told me twenty-five years ago. I'm glad to see you doctors agree on something," Woody told him.

Quite conscientious, the doctor promised him he would never leave Fields' side and even planned to sleep in the same room.

The opening day on the job he staged a question-and-answer session. Sitting with a pad and pen, the doctor began asking questions. The session was short-lived for a very good reason. Here are the only questions I recall:

Question: "When did your drinking first start, Mr. Fields?"
"With a glass of beer."
Question: "Have you ever considered giving up drinking?"
"Why try to improve on happiness?"
Question: "How often do you get drunk?"
"I've been drunk only once in my life." (Then he added, *sotto voce*, understandable only to me: "But that lasted for twenty-three years.")

Young, energetic, and sharp as he was, it proved a hopeless task for the doctor to ferret out all of Woody's hiding places for liquor. Should he discover one and destroy the stock, Woody simply conceived another. His tricks and subterfuges were too much for the physician. When Woody offered to teach the doctor how to play golf, the medico was jubilant. Here, he thought, was one place Fields could never sneak a drink.

Woody appeared for the game dressed in baggy tweed trousers that appeared about two sizes too large. There was a valid reason for his poorly tailored appearance: His pockets were filled with small bottles of whisky, the miniature kind served on trains even today. To protect them from breaking or making a tinkling sound that might arouse the doctor's suspicions, Woody had packed them in cotton wadding.

They started playing. Woody constantly coached the doctor, emphasizing that he should stare at the ball, slowly counting to ten before taking a swing. This gave the coach ample time to sneak a bottle from his pocket and down the contents. A steady stream of instructions kept flowing from teacher to pupil, such as, "Slower, Doc . . . slower, don't look up . . . keep your head down . . . eye on the ball."

After eight days of golfing, the doctor commented, "Mr. Fields, you've been without a drink for quite a spell and you're looking fine."

"Do you really think my health has improved?" Woody asked the doctor.

"One hundred percent," was the answer.

"I'll drink to that," Woody said, forgetting himself and pulling out a bottle.

When it came time to settle the bill, Woody, with his usual business acumen, deducted the golf lessons.

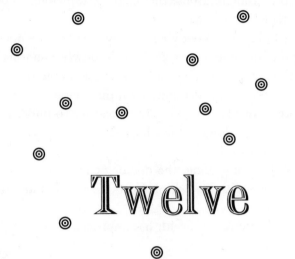

Twelve

I WILL never know whether all Woody's exercising proved beneficial, or merely sharpened his appetite for martinis instead of food. For a month he actually cut down on them after Howard recommended red wine and soda as a tonic. He tried hard, but returned to his beloved gin.

Although the grounds of his residence were capacious, the comedian developed a habit of strolling the roads every evening after dinner, usually wearing a pith helmet. I hardly ever saw him bareheaded when outdoors.

I always accompanied him. Occasionally neighbors would try to strike up a conversation. They didn't get very far—particularly a female celebrity seeker who stopped him, and said, "I see you take a constitutional every evening, Mr. Fields."

Woody mumbled something under his breath.

"You certainly must enjoy walking," the woman prattled.

"I hate it!" He spat out the words.

Surprised, the inquisitive woman asked, "Then why are you walking, Mr. Fields?"

"Because it helps me pass gas after eating," Woody replied, as he brushed her aside with his cane and walked on.

I started to reprimand him, to say something about "disrespect," but thought better of it. What was the use? It would have fallen on deaf ears.

He discouraged still another neighbor from socializing, a tweedy woman who roamed the hills of Laughlin Park. She was the proud mother of a brood of six children, and she bored Woody by telling and retelling some of their *bon mots*.

After three or four of these conversations, the woman guessed, "Somehow, Mr. Fields, I feel that you aren't overly fond of children."

"Only in an experimental way," he said.

"Experimental?" She was puzzled.

"Yes, I have invented something I'd like to try on them."

"Would you care to tell me about it?"

"Gladly, my good woman," he said. "I have invented a permanent gag, adjustable to any size mouth, to fit all children until they reach the age of puberty."

"But how could they eat with their mouths covered?" the neighbor asked.

"They couldn't," Woody stated. "*That*, Madam, is the object of the device. Slow starvation."

Occupying the house behind us was a Mrs. Proust, whose first name I can't recall. She was a great Fields admirer, and every single day for nearly two years would send her Filipino houseboy, Joe, over to invite Woody for a visit. He always declined. She would also cook up special little delicacies, and faithful Joe often appeared with them. None of these unsubtle tricks worked, and Woody steadfastly refused to meet her.

Then, one evening just as he finished eating his fifth gin-marinated olive, a distraught Joe appeared.

"Oh, Mr. Fields," he cried, "Mrs. Proust is dead. On her deathbed she made me promise to bring you to see her."

Woody turned helplessly toward me and his secretary, and his eyes were asking me what to do. "You better honor her last request," I told him.

By this time he was pretty tipsy, and his secretary and I each took him by the arm and followed Joe to the Proust house. It was rather dark inside. The few lights that were burning illuminated suits of armor, which seemed to be everywhere. It was quite spooky.

Mrs. Proust was in the front room, lying in a casket which Joe said had cost $25,000.

"I introduce you," Joe said solemnly. He removed his big white chef's hat, placed it over his heart, faced the casket, and said, "Mrs. Proust, I want you to meet Mr. W.C. Fields, the actor."

Woody bowed low over the casket, started to extend his hand, then quickly pulled it back. "Pleased to make your acquaintance, Madam," he said thickly.

On the way home he went into a fit of raucous laughter. This bizarre episode was far enough removed from the norm to tickle his fancy. Just as we were leaving the Proust front yard, he slipped and tumbled lightly to the ground. He just sat there, and laughed and laughed.

Another close neighbor was Deanna Durbin. Much to Woody's discomfort, we found we were living within range of her voice. Each time she started practicing the scales, he would open the window and shout things like, "Go buy yourself an electric chair!" Sometimes he imitated her in his own harsh voice. Discovering a dying bush and a dead mockingbird on his property, he raved, "Her voice is destroying all flora and fauna in the community. Call the Audubon Society. Call some botany club. If there isn't any, organize one. The woman is a dangerous menace."

In a letter to Miss Durbin, he wrote, "You sound like a squeak through a plugged nostril." I can't remember whether I destroyed it or if it got into the mailbox.

We had no swimming pool on De Mille Drive, but Woody didn't miss it, and he commented that some of his friends would now have to bathe at home and pay their own water bill.

Speaking of water, his doctor told me to try to get him to drink more of it—that it was beneficial to his kidneys. I learned that it was easy enough to lead Woody to water, but not to make him drink. His counter argument was, "Tell me—if water is so important and essential to the human body, why do we wear rubbers, raincoats, and carry umbrellas to avoid it?"

I ordered a gross of bottles of Arrowhead Puritas distilled water, believing he could appreciate the clarity and the chemical-free taste. He took a sip, looked at me, and said, "You know, Chinaman, water does have some value."

It sounded as if he was beginning to see things my way, but his next words destroyed all vestiges of hope.

"If a man is thinking of marrying, he should first give himself the water test: After standing waist deep in an icy stream for ten minutes, when he gets out he'll know if he still wants to get married, or if it was only a rippling of the loins."

I couldn't resist a golden opportunity, and asked, "Suppose you were thinking of me and got into a cold stream. What would happen?"

"I'd freeze my balls off," he replied.

I actually had the temerity to ask him to give up drinking. He regarded me incredulously, and cupped his left hand to his ear as though he didn't hear me correctly.

"Do you realize what you're asking, Chinaman?" he said, raising his eyebrows.

"Yes."

"Great Godfrey!" he exclaimed.

"I mean it, Woody," I said, and added that corny, feminine tag line, "For me."

"For you?"

"For me."

I knew I had him backed into a corner. It was the time for decision. Since he was a man whom I never knew to break his word, all I needed was a simple "okay"—plus willpower. If he did give his assent, it might well add many years to his career and perhaps to his life span.

His answer was, "This calls for a debate."

"I'm not in an argumentative mood, Woody."

"No, no, my dusky love," he said gravely, "not a debate between us."

"Who then?"

"You shall see," he said enigmatically.

With that, he led me to a chair which he placed directly in front of his portable bar. Next, he cleared the bar of everything but a bottle of whiskey, which he positioned squarely in the middle of it.

"Let the playlet begin," he said. "The title is 'Carlotta versus The Bottle.' It is a simple, uncomplicated play with a direct story line. Even La Cava would be able to follow it."

He got behind the bar and sat on the floor, mostly out of sight, and called loudly, "Curtain!"

I was in the front row of the tiny theater of his imagination.

He pointed at the bottle and asked, "Can you sing?"

Then, throwing his voice like his friend Edgar Bergen, and proving to my amazement to be a pretty fair country ventriloquist, Woody made the bottle answer in a high-pitched voice, "No."

Then the dialogue went something like this:

"Can you play the guitar?"

"No," the bottle said.

"Can you talk back to me and give me hell?"

"No."

"But can you give me kisses?" Woody asked.

"Yes."

"That's unheard of."

"No, it isn't. Ever hear of kiss of the hops?"

"Can you make me as happy as Carlotta can?"

"Much happier," the bottle squeaked.

"Can you comfort me like she can? You have no arms."

"I can. She excites you, but I can put you to sleep and she can't."

"You're expendable, but Carlotta isn't," Woody considered. "I admit that."

"I can always pick up the likes of you at any liquor store, but where could I get another Carlotta? Right?"

"Right. On the other hand, where could you get an Old Granddad in a hurry?"

"I can give you up," Woody muttered.

"Yes, I suppose so."

"But I can't give Carlotta up."

"No, you can't."

"Well, then, I've come to the conclusion that I need her worse than I do you. *CURTAIN!*"

I jumped up from the chair, ran over to Woody, and kissed him.

Thoughts were spinning dizzily through my head: He was going to give up drinking for me!

"Let's go out to dinner and celebrate your decision," I proposed.

"Sure," he agreed, "but you'll have to wait until I fix a martini first."

And he made one—triple strength. Well . . . it was an interesting scenario, but not very true to life.

* * * * * * * * * *

One of the first dinner parties held in the De Mille house was a birthday party for me.

That morning he handed me my present, a one-hundred-dollar bill and with it, some philosophy on giving women money: "Give a woman a hundred dollars in small bills and it won't last long. But a hundred-dollar bill she'll hold onto for dear life. She'll keep postponing breaking it. Therefore, you won't have to replenish her coffers for a long time."

Besides myself there was another single girl at the party. She was petite and curvy, and had her eyes on Woody. Of course she hoped this party would be only the beginning.

She evidently didn't know of the existence of a Mrs. Fields (few did, but many suspected). Cornering him where I could hear every word, she asked, "How did such an attractive man as you avoid marriage?"

He patted her on the hand. "By being able to run the hundred-yard dash in ten seconds flat," he answered.

"Oh, Mr. Fields, you're joshing," she said.

He shook his head. "No, my dear. I can furnish you with the names of many cops who will attest to my fleetness of foot."

"Do you know women very well?" she wanted to know.

"I know them backside and foreside. Actually, I have little preference for either side."

"Are you talking about women?"

"I'm not talking about a slab of beef in a butcher shop."

She asked, "What does sex mean to you, Mr. Fields?"

"Today, or thirty years ago?"

"Today."

"Exercise," he answered, "purely exercise, and that is dangerous for an older man. If a girl said 'No' to me, I'd thank her for being so considerate."

The girl gave up, and wiggled away to try her wiles on another good provider.

Woody came over to me and pointed at her. "Remind me never to invite her here again," he said.

He could depend on me.

While I was certainly not a temperance crusader who would smash liquor bottles with an axe, I had a secret weapon that I hoped would prove just as handy in limiting Woody's intake. It was a key to his huge storage room whose specially built shelves contained nearly as many bottles of spirits as a liquor store.

Woody claimed I had "low cunning," and perhaps I did. By peering over his shoulder, I familiarized myself with this one key among the many others he kept on his huge key ring, and one night when I knew he was sleeping heavily (which meant I heard deep snoring), I pilfered his key ring and chain, and stealthily opened the storage room door.

I was really frightened. As I mentioned before, Woody had once given my rump a severe caning and I didn't want a repetition of the act. Anyway, I carted out bottle after bottle, carefully packed them in cardboard boxes, and put them in the Cadillac.

I got up early and went to the car. There was barely room enough for me to squeeze into the driver's seat. Then I headed for the house of a friend of mine—a girl who had made her fame as a Beverly Hills photographer.

"Good lord!" she gasped, "I couldn't drink all that in three lifetimes."

"I know somebody who could in one," I shrugged. "And it will be a lot shorter unless I rid him of these bottles."

"But I really don't want to take them," she persisted.

"Think of it this way," I said. "It's for the good of W.C. Fields."

She sighed resignedly. "For the good of W.C. Fields, then," she said, and we proceeded to stack them in her garage.

Either Woody didn't miss them for two days, or there were enough loose bottles around the house so that it was unnecessary for him to make any pilgrimage to the storage room.

I, needless to say, was on pins and needles waiting for the discovery. When I came home from an afternoon of shopping, he called to me.

"Guess what happened."

Oh, oh, I thought—here it comes.

"Your friend Cathy McCay is certainly a wonderful person."

I already knew that.

He pointed to dozens of bottles stacked in the living room. "Look at the presents she brought me. She didn't even leave a note. Why, if the butler hadn't recognized her, I never would have known who left them. It could have been an anonymous donor." I couldn't believe my ears. "And she knew all my favorite brands," he went on.

I telephoned Cathy. She said her conscience bothered her for two straight nights and she simply had to return the liquor. She had waited until she saw Woody drive away, rang the doorbell, and got the butler and two other servants to carry the bottles back into the house.

There was nothing to do but admit temporary defeat and try something else at a more propitious time.

A month later I believed I had hit on the solution: a psychiatrist. Such a learned and understanding man, with his special knowledge and skills dealing with the human mind, might be just the answer. He could convince Woody of the harm of overdrinking.

For three nights I worked on Woody, and finally he agreed to see one. "If you pay for his coming to the house," he added.

The psychiatrist was expensive enough for a mere office visit —twenty-five dollars hourly—and it was double the price for a house call. After consulting my diminishing bankroll, I prevailed upon an outstanding Beverly Hills doctor to come to De Mille Drive. I admitted the doctor, and then retired to my room, after leaving word with a servant to call me when he was preparing to leave.

One hour and fifty dollars later, the servant knocked on my door. On the way downstairs I really didn't believe I'd hear the sounds of Woody pouring his liquor supply down the drain, but I did have hopes that this would be some sort of beginning of abstinence.

"Any success?" was my burning question to the doctor.

The psychiatrist cleared his throat. "Miss Monti," he said, "in all my years of experience I have never come up against a mind like Mr. Fields'. He is single-minded. Strongly so. It slopes to a single purpose: to drink liquor. I will give you an example. I asked: 'Whom do you love best of all?' His answer to this and every subsequent question was the same: 'Gin.' He doesn't need a doctor, he needs a brewery. And furthermore," the psychiatrist added, "I believe *I* need a drink."

Woody used to say to me, "I hope drinking doesn't change me into a likable character."

This made little sense to me, and I mentioned it to Edgar Bergen.

The ventriloquist, who could probe deeply into a person and understand him, said, "I don't think he wants to change his public image. As you know, he isn't recognized as a very charming and agreeable man with everybody. What's so unusual about him is that he is a *likable* nasty man . . . a likable villain. I think he just plays it a little smarter than anybody. Bill is a smart villain.

"Audiences love his villainy. Do you recall his dialogue with a bartender in *My Little Chickadee?* Fields says, 'You remember the time I knocked down Waterfront Nell?' The bartender answers, 'Why, you didn't knock her down, I did.' And Fields replies: 'Well, I started kicking her first.'

"He has very little public exposure. You don't see him at every benefit and cornerstone laying. And, of course, never at a church. Only his friends and you know him well. You—and I mean the public—see him only where he belongs: on film and in the theater.

"The archives of his mind are loaded with trivia that amuse him and confound others. When we were making *You Can't Cheat an Honest Man* we were going somewhere on location, and he said, 'If we get separated, let us all meet at the Grampian Hills.'

"I wondered about that name, and years later, while traveling in England, I chanced to scan a map of Scotland, and there, between the Lowlands and the Highlands, were the Grampian Hills."

It was during the shooting of *The Bank Dick* that Woody wrote a joke that was later quoted around the United States.

Standing at the cocktail bar, he ordered scotch and a little water chaser. He put his fingers in the water and wiped them on a paper napkin. Then he said to the bartender, "Make it another one, and another chaser. I don't like to bathe in the same water twice."

* * * * * * * * * *

As I have already said, when I first entered his household, Fields was suspicious of my motives, as he was of every woman he ever met.

He told his friend, writer Bill Morrow, about his "acid tests" of my honesty, and how he feigned carelessness by leaving money around the house.

Morrow asked, "How do you know some servant won't steal it?"

"That's a calculated risk I'll have to take," Woody said.

Gradually, through the years, he trusted me more and more, and at last, after repeated testings of my honesty, he discontinued this trick.

Just as I imagined that he trusted me thoroughly, there came a disillusionment.

I was gathering together some of his clothes prior to sending them to the cleaners, and decided to search the pockets for anything he might have forgotten. I came across a pocket that I couldn't seem to open and felt something lumpy inside. Upon closer examination, I found it was sewed shut.

I called his attention to it. He ripped the material open with a penknife and pulled out some currency.

"What in the world does all that mean?" I asked.

He didn't answer.

"Was it a test to see if I'd go into your pockets and take the money?"

"Just an old test, Chinaman," he confessed. "I haven't worn these trousers for two or three years."

"Well, no more tests, please," I requested.

* * * * * * * * * *

I enjoyed being with other women for talk and shopping, but Woody was forever discouraging me from seeing them. One friend, with her sister and mother, rented a house in Laguna Beach and invited me down. I told Woody, and he was reluctant to let me go. Finally he consented, placing a time limit of three days on the visit. I asked him if I could take my hostesses some food from our well-stocked larder, as I didn't have enough money at the moment to bring a present.

"No," he refused. "I'm not going to put my food in alien stomachs."

Pleadings failed to dissuade him, and I became angry. Getting up early in the morning of the Laguna trip, I went into the pantry and loaded the car with food, including several bottles of wine. Why not? I rationalized. Woody was a millionaire and ought to be a little more charitable.

By seven, I was carrying the last item, an eighteen-pound ham, out to the car. Now I am no weakling, and eighteen pounds is not an excessively heavy burden to bear, but a woman never knows when one of her heels is liable to catch on something—mine got hung up on the ninth stair from the bottom.

The ham and I became airborne, both making rough unscheduled landings. The result: three broken ribs and a vertebra out of place.

Della came runnning to help pick me up. She looked at me worriedly and said, "Miss Carlotta, your condition seems mighty bad."

I told her it felt that way.

She helped me to the car. I could scarcely walk. I drove slowly to Beverly Hills where I was to meet my friend, and the two of us took off for Laguna Beach. The pain worsened. My friend insisted I get right to a hospital. I gave her the food and liquor, sent my regrets to her mother and sister, and hoped she would enjoy herself. She refused to leave until she drove me to the Queen of Angels Hospital, where I was taken inside on a stretcher.

Woody came to the hospital immediately.

"I won't lecture to you and say 'the way of the transgressor is hard,' " he commented, "nor will I say that 'honesty is the best policy' because I've never believed that myself. I don't have to say a word. The ham has done all the talking for me."

He made a really dramatic incident out of what happened. Four days later, when I was home again, I heard him tell Bill Morrow, "Yes sir, the Chinaman was stealing a ham from me. She was going to take all the money and jewelry in the house and hide out, but she needed a ham for sustenance. A ham can keep you alive for a month. You can't trust the Chinese. They always speak of their 'honorable ancestors,' but this proves that what goes on in the family tree is a dastardly lie."

Morrow knew me well, as well as Woody's nickname for me, but asked, "Why, Bill, I thought she was of Latin extraction?"

"Latin . . . Chinese . . . what's the difference? It's only a matter of geography," Woody said.

But his tightness and his generosity were inconsistent. Once we motored down the coast to the Delmar racetrack where we met Bing Crosby. Bing gifted Woody with a beautiful and powerful pair of binoculars that nearly brought the horses into your lap.

I didn't know much about the races, but the colors of one of the jockeys gave me an intuitive flash—which any veteran bettor will tell you is the worst kind. I asked Woody if he would give me some money to bet on the horse of my choice in the second race.

"Not one cent to wager," he stated resolutely.

At the same time he handed me the recently acquired binoculars. "Take them," he insisted. "They're all yours."

I took them—and watched my horse finish first.

Although Woody already had a Cadillac and two Lincolns in his garage, he purchased still another car—a station wagon—the make of which escapes me.

"I need it for sporting events," was his excuse.

Into this wagon would pour (and I can't think of a more appropriate word) Gene Fowler, Roland Young, Greg La Cava, Jack La Rue, John Barrymore and Jack Oakie, bound for football games at the Rose Bowl or Jeffries' Barn—a fight arena in the San Fernando Valley operated by the former heavyweight champion, Jim Jeffries.

In a 1940 Rose Bowl encounter when Southern California tangled with Tennessee, the Fields group kept chanting, "We want Quackenbush! . . . We want Quackenbush!" Before long approximately two thousand fans took up the cry and many were seen riffling through their programs attempting to find the name.

A woman sitting behind Woody tapped him on the shoulder asking, "Just who is Quackenbush?"

"One of the greatest players alive," the comedian answered. "A real four-threat man."

"I thought it was triple-threat," the woman said. "Punt, pass and run."

"And drink," Woody quickly added. He pointed to the Tennessee bench. "See the boy sitting by the water bucket?"

"Yes."

"That's Quackenbush and that bucket's loaded with Tennessee sour mash liquor."

"But—but," the woman said, confused, "isn't that against the rules?"

"Normally yes," Woody answered, "but the boy's father is the owner of a giant distillery, so they make an exception." He tipped his hat and resumed the throaty cry of "We want Quackenbush!"

This sporting group never lasted longer than the first quarter at which time they exited to the station wagon to drink and follow the remainder of the game on the radio. Once for privacy they pitched a tent to set up a bar. Fields was standing in front of the tent when a matronly woman passing by inquired, "What is the purpose of this, sir?"

"An emergency woman's rest room," he explained, "for those who can't hold it until they reach the stadium."

Just then La Cava and Fowler came out.

"What—what are those men doing in there?" the woman gasped.

"Transvestites, madam," Woody replied.

Thirteen

I N the street, in the stores, nowhere in public did people associate me with W.C. Fields. Behind my back there were no whispers, "Oh, that's Carlotta Monti," nor even, "Don't look now, but there goes W.C. Fields' girl friend."

I was just another passer-by, until the *Hollywood Citizen News* ran a picture of me on page one with the overhead caption: SHE DENIES ROMANCE WITH COMEDIAN.

The text read: "Carlotta Monti, Spanish-Italian screen dancer appearing in Sam Goldwyn's film *Barbary Coast*, denied today that she and W.C. Fields contemplate marriage. She admitted she has been seen with the comedian often in the last eleven months. She pointed out that Mr. Fields has a wife in New York, though they have been separated many years."

I thought little of it until I kept a dental appointment. In the past, taking pity on me because of my low income, the dentist had always charged me a nominal fee. Now, from the moment I went into his office, he treated me with more respect than in the past.

Just as I was climbing into the dental chair, he stopped me and called to his assistant, "Miss Cain, will you please dust off the chair? Miss Monti is wearing a blue suit and I don't want it to pick up any lint."

During the course of filling a molar he repeatedly asked, "Is the drill bothering you?" Formerly, if he hit a nerve and I jumped, he kept silent. All these changes mystified me—until I asked the office girl on the way out how much I owed.

She told me, and I couldn't believe it. His prices had tripled since my last visit, and these were not inflationary times.

"There must be some mistake."

I waited while she consulted the dentist, who sent the girl back with the following cryptic message: "You're a celebrity now." The translation was simple. And I might say I got the message loud and clear.

If I thought this was unjust . . ! When my friend Cathy McCay came in for a tooth pulling, she was charged double the usual price: "Why the increase in prices?" Cathy asked. "Because you're a friend of Carlotta Monti," the dentist answered.

Cathy telephoned me that evening. "We've been friends for a long time," she began. "But honestly, Carlotta, *I don't know if I can afford it any longer.*"

The high cost of publicity continued to afflict me. I had a wonderfully cheap dressmaker who I didn't think ever read a newspaper. But I was wrong, and her fees doubled. Meanwhile, my credit rating soared. Three people called to borrow money at no interest rates.

I told Woody jokingly, "I'm not sure I can afford to live here any longer. My prosperity is getting me down."

"I'll tell you what I'm going to do, my beautiful one," he said, "I'm going to put you in my will for $50,000."

I thought he was kidding, until the following week when his lawyer came to the house and he drew up a new will. He called me into his office to show me a copy, whereby I was to inherit $50,000 when he died. I started to cry, not only on account of gratitude, but because I hated to think of wills and talk about his death.

He dried my eyes with a white silk handkerchief. "No tears," he said, "to water those dusky cheeks."

I dabbed at my eyes with some tissue, and put the legacy from my mind.

Whenever possible (which was most of the time), Woody conducted varied matters of business directly from his house. A shirtmaker, a shoemaker, clothiers, and various tradespeople would come in to save him from making public appearances. One of his women servants acted as laundress.

I tried to screen the calls people made on him. One day I slipped up when a life insurance salesman came to the door, claiming that he had an appointment. I ushered him in to Woody's office and lolled in the background. Sometimes it was tantamount to a postgraduate course to hear the way Fields dealt with people.

The salesman, young and hardhitting, opened a briefcase of charts and figures, spreading the printed sheets on Woody's desk.

Woody regarded them distastefully. "Don't distract me with the facts," he said, and proceeded to argue on why he didn't need a policy. He concluded, and glared at the young man.

"No one can live forever, Mr. Fields," was the salesman's reminder.

"When you grow a little older," Woody countered, "you'll learn that no one wants to."

The resolute pitchman was full of clichés: "Life is a gamble," he said.

Woody retorted, "I don't gamble unless I have the edge."

"Give up drinking, and you will have," the salesman remarked.

I gave an imperceptible start. Right then and there I could see this presumptuous young man had just eliminated any possibility of a sale.

I was anxious to hear Woody's reaction. But he sat in silence.

Believing his argument had struck home, the salesman tossed Woody the policy and said, "Just put your John Hancock on the dotted line, Mr. Fields."

Woody signed it with a flourish. I gasped: Was he getting soft or had an early stage of senility arrived? The salesman picked up the contract, a victorious grin on his face. He soon lost it.

"Mr. Fields," he said, studying the signature, "is this some kind of joke?"

Woody seemed puzzled. "Joke?" he echoed.

"Yes. You signed the contract 'John Hancock.' "

"Well, isn't that what you asked me to do?"

His spirits crushed, the salesman began breathing heavily, almost raspingly, a wheezing admission of defeat. In a voice that sounded like the cacophony of the bass section of a symphony orchestra that couldn't read music, Woody began a scathing attack against both the salesman's profession and the rock-ribbed business institution he represented. For a full ten minutes the tirade continued unabated. As his voice reached a crescendo, he paused to inhale.

His antagonist had been rocked back on his heels by the blast. Now was a chance for him to squeeze in a quick sentence, and he said, "A soft answer turneth away wrath, Mr. Fields."

"It does?" Woody innocently inquired.

"Yes sir," the salesman responded.

"Well, here's one then," Woody said, and he whispered, "Fuck you and your company and kindly get the hell off my property!"

I escorted a crestfallen salesman to the door. Before he left he said to me, "He's a very difficult man. How can you stand living with him?"

"It's easy when you love someone," I informed him.

The only time I ever knew a life insurance salesman to

score with him was when an older representative approached Fields. It was a fast deal.

Woody asked, "Would you care for a drink?"

"I'd love one," the salesman replied.

"What's your pleasure?" Woody asked.

"A strong martini with an olive," the man answered. (Evidently he had done his research well.)

Woody made the drink and shook the salesman's hand. "You're a man after my own heart," he complimented, "and it's going to be a pleasure to do business with you." Several martinis later he took out a modest policy.

Many people have asked me how I mixed martinis for Woody, everyone expecting a secret formula or something different in the way of a special technique of making them. Not so. I simply put a lot of cracked ice into a big pitcher, used six parts gin to one part dry vermouth, stirred briskly, poured, and dropped an olive or an onion speared on a toothpick into the glass.

Mack Sennett—whose real name was Michael Sinott—John Barrymore, and John Decker were his most capacious drinking companions. The exchanges of dialogue among this quartet should have been recorded for posterity. But I do remember that in his jousts against the other minds, Sennett always finished last.

I also remember Woody expostulating on the value of friendship: "I've been barbecued, stewed, screwed, tattooed, and fried by people claiming to be friends. The human race has gone backward, not forward, since the days we were apes swinging through the trees."

At another session, arguments were raging on doctors' and lawyers' value to society, one of Woody's favorite topics. He told his three companions of the bottle, "Don't ever make the mistake of going to see a doctor on the day the stock market drops, because he'll try to recover his losses on your bill."

Concerning lawyers: "The only thing a lawyer won't question is the legitimacy of his own mother."

Although he spoke in glowing terms of London audiences during his juggling days, he took periodic digs at the English. "All Englishmen," he told Decker, Barrymore, and Sennett, talk as if they've got a bushel of plums stuck in their throats, and then after swallowing them got constipated from the pits."

From time to time, when intoxicated—and, as I've said before, this condition never was revealed in his walk or talk —he fired servants, only to rehire them the next day. During his affiliation with Edgar Bergen and Charlie McCarthy on the *Chase and Sanborn Hour* radio show, he fired his chauffeur. I asked him why, since Woody always had admired the man's driving.

"For a valid reason," he explained. "He was listening to his radio."

"Is anything wrong with that?" I asked.

"There certainly is," he said vehemently. "The sonofabitch is going to listen to my program or none at all. One of my spies reported he was tuned to another network while I was on the air."

In the De Mille house he engaged expert electronics men to install a giant "bugging" system, wiring every room and placing a master switch in his office so he could listen in or amplify his voice nearly anywhere in the house if he so chose. Some of the speakers were even concealed behind ivy that covered the red-tiled lane which bisected the green lawn and led to the house. As you entered this walk there was a sign: MARPLE HALL. I never found out its origin, but despite severe buffetings in the weather, it is still visible today.

Once Woody and I were sitting in his office awaiting a nationally syndicated female gossip columnist and her escort, who were coming to dinner. When he heard the slamming of a car door, which signaled that a 200-foot walk would soon begin for the arrivals, he turned on the intercom system and picked up the voice of the columnist, who spoke roughly but only in private.

"I wonder what the drunken old sonofabitch is doing right now?"

Before her escort could answer, Woody's snarling voice boomed through the ivy, "The old sonofabitch isn't home, and if he is, he's too drunk to see you!"

There were two empty places for dinner that evening.

Another time when guests were making their way toward the house, he spied a stray dog in the yard near his roses. Of course the speaker system was turned on again when he shouted, "Either shit, pee, or get off the grounds."

Probably my worst embarrassment occurred as I was taking some friends on a tour of the estate. Woody was lying on the grass, gazing skyward. I thought he was fast asleep. I wish he had been. Spotting a bird flying low overhead, he snarled, "I know what you're up to, you white-feathered fiend. Go release your bowels on some lesser personage."

Speaking of dinner, Mack Sennett fancied himself quite a cook. Actually, he was fantastically rotten, but there was no stopping him; he insisted on fixing dinner for us. He boiled everything until it was tasteless, and it was usually ham, beef, and cabbage, prompting Woody to remark, "If they bottled his cooking and dropped it over Germany, the war would come to a sudden ending."

A pompous man who was used to giving orders to Charlie Chaplin, Fatty Arbuckle, Marie Dressler, and bevies of bathing beauties in films he directed for his Keystone Company, Sennett seldom took no for an answer from anyone. If he felt like cooking, no one could argue him out of it. To prevent him from mutilating the food and to discourage his cooking, Woody would ply him with martinis. Watching Sennett gulp them down, he whispered to me, "If I can only get him boiled, he'll forget about boiling everything else."

Such good luck, though, was virtually impossible to achieve. Only once did we escape his spreading mass indigestion.

While working up an appetite for cooking, Sennett was

walking under an olive tree on Woody's lawn, when a close friend of Woody's who was gifted with occult powers, Mrs. Ethel Rice, called to him. "Stop! I have a message for you from Mabel Normand." She termed it an "ectoplasmic manifestation."

Mabel Normand, a star directed by Sennett in silent pictures, had been dead for many years. She had never gotten along with the comedy maker, and they were always engaged in ferocious verbal fights.

Sennett stopped dead in his tracks and faced Mrs. Rice. "What did she say?" he asked.

"She said to tell Mack Sennett that he's an old bastard and that she'll never forgive him."

The color drained from Sennett's face. He strode to his car and drove rapidly away.

"One man's fears are the good fortune of others," Woody commented. "Tonight our stomachs have been spared."

I recently drove out to see Ethel Rice and her daughter, lawyer Joan Martin who now represents me. Of course the conversation swung to Woody, and Mrs. Rice said, "The side of him I knew was that of a charming host. He was a man who tried to please. He loved to perform little niceties for people and he made you feel better for having spent an hour with him. Mr. Fields had a giving heart. I always came away feeling that I'd gained something. Nothing ever spoiled a visit with him."

When I was singing at Santa Barbara at the El Paseo, Ethel came up to drive me back to De Mille Drive the day the engagement ended. A policeman gave her a ticket for speeding, and of all streets to have it happen on, it was coincidentally named Ethel.

I told Woody, and he paid the fine and sent Ethel the receipt and a membership to the Automobile Club of Southern California. "I have great admiration for her," Woody said. "After all, wasn't she breaking the law to hurry you back to me?"

When Ethel and Joan were going to Cuba, Woody cautioned

them not to waste time wandering around Havana searching for tourist attractions. "The only two sights worth seeing," he insisted, "are the Tropicana Brewery and the rum distillery."

* * * * * * * * * *

Actor Patrick Knowles and I were good friends. He had his picture taken with Irene Dunne on his lap, and later a photographer got hold of it and transposed my head on Irene's body. It was a splendid job of trick photography. But a man from Universal who wasn't overly fond of Woody showed it to him, and Fields went into a tantrum.

That afternoon before I returned from shopping, he threw all my clothes out onto the lawn. It was impossible to reason with him.

At this very time the Metropolitan Opera Company was scheduled to perform *Boris Godunoff* and *La Boheme* at the Los Angeles Shrine Auditorium, featuring Ezio Pinza and Lily Pons. My singing teacher, Alexia Bassian, who had sung with Arturo Toscanini at Covent Garden, London, telephoned to offer me a role in the chorus. The part called for me to wear a peasant costume and put my hair into long braids.

As I ruefully surveyed my clothes pitched onto the grass, I thought how providentially timed this opportunity was; doing something I loved would redeem me in his eyes.

By the time I told Woody about the offer, my anger had cooled somewhat.

"How much are they paying my little unfaithful thrush?" he asked sarcastically.

"Two dollars," I said.

"A minute, I presume."

"Not exactly," I said hesitatingly.

"How much?" he demanded.

"A performance," I answered sheepishly.

He laughed until his eyes were wet with tears. I knew a way to make him stop, so I said, "Ezio Pinza is in the company."

His laughter faded. Pinza and I were firm friends, and Woody had always felt jealous of him. "That dastardly troubador," he snarled. "May he get permanent laryngitis."

He raised his cane. Frightened, I ran into the house.

The upshot of it was that I sang in the chorus for six nights. Although the composite photo had caused a temporary rupture in our relations, I still had not told him the truth inasmuch as I felt he should have trusted me. He did not object to my taking his Cadillac to the opera and parking it in a lot across the street during the performance where they charged me a dollar.

Every night when I came home, Woody had clippings and photos of Pinza cut out and pasted on the mirror of my dressing table, and each night I would tear them off. I didn't tell him that Pinza had complimented me and waxed rapturous over my appearance.

The opera concluded its run, and Woody called me into his office. "I want you to be a witness to something," he said.

I asked what it was.

"Practically to your indigent old age," he said.

Then he went on to explain that he had taken me out of his will, and instead of receiving $50,000, I was now to get nothing.

It was contemptible of him to do this and I demanded to know what motivated his actions.

"First, your singing," he said.

"Please explain."

"You know how I hate singing," he reminded, "and still you went downtown for six nights and sang your lungs out. You made twelve dollars. You told me it cost you a dollar per night to park. Well, you lost $49,994, if you follow my arithmetic."

"It was worth it," I retaliated, furious.

It was then, for the first time, that I told him how false his suspicions were and pointed out that trick photography was used to make it appear that I was sitting on Patrick Knowles' lap. I kept getting angrier as I thought this over in retrospect, and concluded by declaring I was going to sue someone—most likely the nimble-fingered photographer.

I contacted my lawyer and filed suit. That evening Woody, Joan, and Ethel Rice tried to coach me. Woody put me through some cross-examinations, and when it ended said, "For heaven's sake, settle out of court for anything you can get; otherwise you'll end up in Tehachapi [the California State Women's Prison]."

Acting upon his advice, I abandoned the case.

The strain on our relationship eased and Woody became tender again. He gave me a present, a stuffed bird ornament with beautiful feathers that I was supposed to wear in my hair. According to advertisements, they were featuring them in an exclusive Wilshire Boulevard store at a price of $575.

"Wear it in good health and bad voice," he advised, "and let it be a lesson to you. This bird also used to sing, like someone I know—and look what it got her."

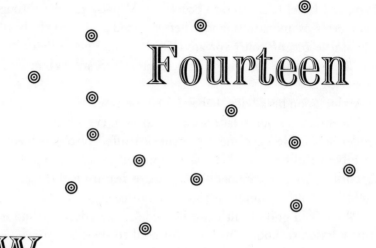

Fourteen

WOODY once confessed that he was worth a million, three hundred thousand dollars. "That is," he qualified, "before anyone starts a lawsuit against me." He was deathly afraid of lawsuits, so much so, in fact, that he was fearful to open his daily mail.

Woody admitted having lost "a tidy sum" in 1929 when the stock market nose-dived, but so far as I could sense, he had dismissed the debacle from his mind and did a minimum of brooding.

"Those hit hardest were committing suicide by jumping out of windows," he recalled, adding, "I did likewise on that fatal day."

I asked in amazement, "You tried suicide?"

"Oh no," he corrected, "not suicide. I jumped from a first-floor window to avoid a jealous husband who came home unexpectedly."

"But you must have grieved for a while over stock losses," I guessed.

"Only a trifle. Never cry over spilt milk, because it may have been poisoned."

Soon after I moved into his house he made it plain to me that he was never going to give me any large sums of money. I was satisfied, asking for nothing for myself.

He must have felt guilty, however, for he said, "Money means nothing to you. You'd become a philanthropist if I gave you anything but a pittance. The trouble with you, Chinaman, is that you're too goodhearted."

"Thanks," I said.

"Show me a bank balance, and I'll tell you if that person is a success. What's yours?" he asked.

I knew it to the penny. "Thirty-seven dollars and forty-five cents," I revealed.

He scratched the back of his head with his cane. Then, giving me the benefit of the doubt, "Well, perhaps you're a success in other ways."

A cousin of mine became sick, and after a month of doctor bills, he was running out of money. This was one of the few times I ever asked Woody for anything monetary. He refused. The sickness kept preying on my mind. I had no choice but to sell my furniture in storage and settle the medical bills. But his recovery more than repaid me.

I often chided Woody about his penuriousness, pointing out that he was living in a mansion with nine servants, had seven cars, and was working at a cheap, scarred, ink-stained desk of an outmoded rolltop style.

"It's satisfactory," he contended, "and furthermore, if I want to write down a joke and can't find a pencil, there's a penknife in the drawer that I can use to carve the words into the wood."

"The desk is too ratty for you. Treat yourself to a new one." I kept arguing until he became angry and trumpeted, "Quiet, girl who speaks with an adder's tongue!"

I was passing a store on Broadway in downtown Los Angeles and noticed some exquisite desks for sale. Naturally, the one I was attracted to was the most expensive, priced at $5,000. I knew Woody would hit the ceiling—and perhaps even me—if I dared suggest that he buy it. I mentioned to the salesman that I thought it was greatly overpriced, and he said, "I'll let you have it for $3,500."

Elated, I rushed to the telephone to relay the sensational news to Woody, and verbally patted myself on the back, for some shrewd bargaining.

He mulled it over. "So the bandits came down from $5,000 to $3,500," he mused.

"Yes," I said, bubbling enthusiastically, "isn't it wonderful? Shall I buy it?"

"Hold on, woman," he said. Admitting that it sounded like a fine piece of furniture, after some deliberation, he instructed me, "Offer them $1,500."

"I haven't got the nerve," I gasped.

"Try it."

Oh, well, I thought, the worst that can happen is that I'll get insulted and kicked out of the store. So I said bravely to the salesman, "I'll give you $1,500 for the desk."

To my surprise, he said, "It's a deal, lady—and a real bargain."

At the beginning of World War II, Woody, through reading, listening, and his own opinions, was certain that many shortages would occur to deprive buyers of the necessities of life. Before this happened, he planned to hoard by starting a one-man buying spree. For some reason, eggs popped into his mind, although he ate them only infrequently. Nothing could discourage him from purchasing every egg within a radius of several square miles. His entire staff was pressed into service, and by the day's end he had accumulated thousands, which he stored in the basement.

"But, Woody," I kept arguing, "they'll spoil."

He said, "Nonsense. We'll use them up in a hurry. Remind me to have one for breakfast tomorrow."

Barrymore came over to dinner, and Woody, proud of his accumulation, took the actor to the basement to exhibit gleefully the results of his shopping. "Good heavens!" Barrymore exclaimed, "Where in the name of the devil did all those eggs come from?"

"From a hen's ass, you fool!" Woody snapped.

Barrymore was gifted with a dozen. As I picked up the carton to hand it to him, the top slipped open and an egg fell out, breaking on the floor.

Woody's face flushed with anger. He bawled me out for carelessness.

"It's only one out of thousands," I reminded him.

"True enough," he agreed, "but it could have been the one that might have hatched and helped us start a new crop."

Despite the fact that a close link of friendship, forged over the years, existed between Jack Barrymore and Woody, it wasn't always like that. They had once been bitter rivals for the affection of Nora Bayes, the musical comedy singer whose voice charmed all within range. Some wag called their yearning for Miss Bayes "The Great Profile vs. The Putty Nose."

Barrymore couldn't shake off his rival, who clung to Miss Bayes with the indomitable spirit of a terrier, so he decided to confront Fields and talk it over. He believed he had staked out a prior claim on Miss Bayes and that Woody was invading his territory.

There were rumors along Broadway that a fight was in the offing. Should they have decided on a duel with a choice of weapons, I always thought it would be martini pitchers at twenty paces.

At any rate, they talked it over. The outcome was that Barrymore stated, "I fell in love with Mr. Fields and didn't care any more about Miss Bayes."

A member of the Coor family, the Colorado brewers, prophesied that a scarcity of beer was bound to hit the nation, due to the war. Woody grew genuinely alarmed. About once every year he tried to taper off the hard stuff by hitting the beer, and even to think it might be hard to secure was alarming. Therefore, the next day he purchased two hundred cases, which he locked in the storage room with a vast array of gin, whisky, rum, brandy, vermouth, and various wines.

Observing a cot in the middle of all the bottled stock, I asked its purpose.

"For a guard to sleep on, if I hire one," he answered.

Both the beer and the eggs aged, but it was the latter the neighbors complained of, as fetid odors swept the air over the private park.

When a woman accosted him on the street and demanded to know if he were running a slaughter house, he informed her, "We're under gas attack by the enemy. Rumor hath it that the Nazis have landed at Santa Monica."

At the beginning of the war he bought a huge wall map and boxes of different colored thumbtacks, and would record the daily progress of the Allied forces and the Nazis.

One night he pushed a thumbtack into his hand, staining part of France red. I went for a cold, wet towel to wipe off the crimson blot, but he wouldn't let me. "If the Nazis keep advancing in the same direction they are now moving, there is liable to be a big battle right where the blood is." It was more realistic that way.

If Woody were in one of his chauvinistic moods, trampling one blade of grass on his lawn without invitation, invited the same dangers as wandering haphazardly over a mine field. In the gathering dusk of one warm evening Woody spied a helmeted figure, flashlight in hand, cutting across the lawn toward his house. Woody rushed downstairs, horse pistol in hand, threw open the door, drew a bead on the approaching person, and shouted, "Halt!"

The man came to a jarring stop.

"Hands up!" Woody cried.

With his hands in the air, the man called, "I'm Cecil B. De Mille."

"That's not the password," Woody informed, and threatened, "Give the right one or I'll fill you full of lead."

The boss of Paramount Studios tried to establish his identity by declaring, "I'm your neighborhood air raid warden."

"Can you prove it?" Woody wanted to know, pointing out, "You're wearing a German helmet."

"It's an air raid helmet," De Mille insisted.

"We haven't had any air raids."

"It's a preventive measure."

Woody was not going to be taken in so easily. "Maybe you're an aged paratrooper. One who's been lost for many years."

"Listen, I'm . . ."

"You speak English well for a Nazi," he complimented. "Where did you learn our language?"

"I was born here."

"Oh, a traitor to your country," Woody ranted. "Another Benedict Arnold. There's a noose waiting for the neck of the likes of you."

Suddenly Woody fired a warning shot into the air. De Mille jumped nervously. When he could find his voice again, he reminded him, "I pay your salary, you know."

"Leave a check in the mailbox and beat a hasty retreat," Woody advised.

De Mille wasn't accustomed to having anyone within a hundred feet of him who wasn't in complete agreement. He shook his head incredulously and stated his reason for the visit. The blinds, he said, must be drawn tightly over all windows at night because a light would tend to give aid and comfort to the enemy in case of air attack, and neighbors had said that lights were streaming from the Fields windows far into the night.

"Mind your own studio, and I'll take care of my own windows," Woody stubbornly replied.

Visibly shaken from the experience, the studio boss trudged home. From that day on, De Mille's male secretary relieved him of his air raid warden duties.

"Fosselized old curmudgeon," Woody mumbled, returning to the house. He handed his pistol to a servant with the instructions, "Clean my fetlock and be sure it's in working order. The marauders are closing in on us."

When we dined at Chasen's that evening he told the restauranteur, "I damned near shot him. I mistook him for a bald eagle. *Haliaeetus lecocephalus,* as you no doubt are aware. A most ferocious bird of prey."

"How did you know it wasn't really an eagle?" Chasen asked, stringing along with the story.

"Why, I looked him squarely in the eye," Woody recounted, "and I saw the reflections of thousands of extras from his spectacle pictures."

Woody obstinately refused to black out his window lights, which brought a call from the police to enforce the law. A sergeant and a lieutenant were sent to see him.

The lieutenant opened the conversation. "Mr. Fields, we have received several complaints about you."

"If they didn't like my picture, why didn't they get their money back from the box-office, and stop running to the police?" Woody countered.

"It ain't that . . ." the sergeant began, only to have his superior officer cut in with, "I'll take over, Jim."

"You boys care for a shot?" Woody asked.

"We're not allowed to drink on duty," the lieutenant said.

"Bah!" Woody snorted, "That's the trouble with you gendarmes. Failure to take advantage of a good situation."

"We're here regarding your windows," the lieutenant said. "You don't pull the curtains at night."

Woody pointed a finger at the officer. "Are you accusing me of being an exhibitionist?"

"No, no," the lieutenant said hastily. "It's the blackout. It's unlawful to allow lights to show through windows. I hope you'll comply with the regulations, sir."

"The country is choked with meaningless regulations."

"This one is enforceable," the lieutenant reminded.

Woody finally complied.

Later he sneered, "Police are the menace of the free world." And he reminisced, "I should have shot De Mille in the first place. He was a trespasser and I had my constitutional rights."

* * * * * * * * * *

He was eating less and less solid food. In all my years with him, I had never known him to eat a hearty meal. Vainly, I tried to get him to start the day off with something nourishing.

One morning when he arose before me and I asked him about breakfast, he answered, "My appetite was ravenous this morning."

I inquired what he had eaten.

"A piece of toast."

"Only toast?"

"No," he said. "It had butter on it."

Days when he was not working at a studio he sated his restlessness by prowling the grounds of the estate, keeping a sharp lookout for marauders, a weather eye trained at the sky, and an ear tuned for possible vocal outpourings from the Deanna Durbin residence.

He had a special interest in flowers, and often remarked, "Chinaman, I want you to keep my drunken friends from breathing on the roses."

Keeping accurate track of his drinking was an impossibility. Even a computer might have tossed in the sponge. As near as I could figure, he was consuming close to two quarts of martinis daily. At no particular time did he drink more or less, maintaining a steady, 'round-the-clock cocktail hour.

"You should have married a martini," I once told him after being upset at something or other.

He shook his head. "Too cold, my dear. None of the warmth that your hot Spanish blood furnishes."

People still ask me, "Was W.C. Fields romantic?"

I don't think it matters to the public. He established a

reputation for comedy, not sex. If you want sex, you think of reading Harold Robbins, Philip Roth, or Jacqueline Susann. If you think of comedy you think of Fields.

Of course we had a romance. He was as much a perfectionist in his lovemaking as he was in his juggling. He never dropped a cigar box accidentally, and by the same token he never fumbled during a golden moment.

Still, quite early in our relationship, as the flame that once ran through his loins was gradually reduced to some faintly glowing embers, I began to think that in the run for his affections, the martini pitcher came first, the icebox second, and yours truly an outdistanced third. Naturally his virility drowned as his libido became soaked in alcohol. And it didn't go down the customary three times, it just sank.

At the studios, friends would try to drag him into the commissary for lunch, but he preferred dining as a loner in his dressing room, close to his gin and vermouth. His favorite luncheon dish was crabmeat salad—and half a portion was his capacity, washed down by a martini.

"The martini," he told Eddie Sutherland, "resuscitates the crabs and gives them a final fling at life before being buried forever in a vault of stomach."

Among his many utterances on the subject of liquor, I can recall him saying, "The proper drink for each individual comes only after much study and experimentation. For my part, I have tried everything offered by the distillers and brewers. Each one affects me differently. Some cause lack of sleep; others, drowsiness; a few make me hot; two or three make me cold. One of them, bourbon, makes me drunk.

"In the long run, and for a continuation drink—and by that I mean twenty-four hours—give me martinis. They work fast, and the sensations are lasting. They prick my mind like the cut of a razor blade. I work better with them inside me.

"The martini is a purely American concoction, originating during the Gay Nineties. It was first made at New York's

Waldorf-Astoria, and named after a New Orleans gentleman, Mr. Martinez."

"And made famous by a Mr. W.C. Fields," I concluded.

On another, but related, subject, he said, "The worst disease known to man, and one neglected by medical science, is 'Martini Elbow.' It's a cousin to 'Tennis Elbow' but more severe. Painful calcium deposits make it impossible for the unfortunate drinker to lift his cocktail glass. He must, therefore, either have an assistant with him to perform this duty, or he must himself bend his face down to the glass—a dangerous procedure, as the glass rim may cut his proboscis."

Everything else having failed to divorce him from liquor, I even did the childish thing of having him raise his right hand and solemnly swear never to take a drink again. The time of this historic event was four o'clock on a summer afternoon in 1945. Two hours later I saw him downing a martini.

"You swore off," I accused. "You took a sacred oath."

He admitted such had been the case. "But," he said childishly, "I didn't say for how long."

His doctor put him on one martini per day. Woody readily agreed. How was the medic to know the "one" drink was one long one—from a full two-quart shaker?

I was, however, successful in making him quit cigars. I felt jubilant until one day I commented, "Doesn't non-smoking improve your health? Don't you really feel healthier?" He said, "I certainly do. With no cigar in my mouth, my mouth is always ready to receive a drink."

In those days, and earlier, kids worshipped a number of actors who stood for clean living. The cigar-smoking heroes, anxious not to lose a single fan, invariably held their cigars behind their backs or tossed them away at the approach of youngsters. Ken Maynard, the cowboy star who was so clean in his movies he must have been antiseptically scrubbed and rarely even got to kiss a girl, was one of this fraternity.

Not so W.C. Fields. Although he didn't attract many

adolescents seeking autographs—mainly because they were his oppressors in his pictures—if they did approach him, he made no effort to dispose of his long cigar. In fact, I saw him blow a suffocating cloud of smoke into the face of one youngster; the boy sprinted away, coughing violently.

"How could you?" I berated him.

"I am teaching him a lesson on the evils of smoking," was his explanation, "besides getting rid of the junior knave."

At another time a child asked him how old he was when he started smoking. He answered the question with a question: "How old are *you*, sonny?"

"I'm eight."

"Eight . . . eight," he mused. "Ah yes, I remember. Eight was the exact age I became addicted to the weed." Handing the child a cigar, he walked away.

It was useless to reprimand him.

Mack Sennett, Eddie Sutherland, Greg La Cava, Bill LeBaron, and scores of others agreed that Woody delivered his lines better when drinking. They said it improved his timing. Barrymore said, "Alcohol is a blessing, not in disguise, to him."

Added to a list of Woody's pet hatreds were the Germans and the Japanese of World War II. Anyone he met whose eyes were not considered normal by American optical standards, he imagined to be a Nipponese spy. Likewise, a person with an accent whose identity he couldn't fathom qualified as a German agent.

He was certain that the delivery boy from a liquor store he patronized was a German juvenile spy—"just learning the business," as he put it. He called the store owner on the telephone to seek information on the youngster's background.

"His father was in a concentration camp and so was the boy," Woody was told.

Hating to admit he was wrong, Woody showed his stubborn streak. "Are you positive?" he persisted.

"I've seen numbers tattooed on him, Mr. Fields."

Woody pondered over this and requested, "Do me a favor, Max, and see if they wash off with laundry soap and water. A citizen can't be too cautious these days. Say!" he suddenly demanded, "Isn't Max a German name?"

"Why, yes, it is," the man admitted.

"I'm surrounded by a network of spies," Woody said helplessly, and after hanging up, diverted his future business to a store operated by an Irish proprietor.

"If I hadn't changed, I might have been drugged," he claimed.

Southern California was hard pressed for adequate gardeners during the war years, as authorities rounded up the Japanese colony and clapped them into a High Sierra retreat called Manzanar.

Woody ran an advertisement in a newspaper for a gardener. I interviewed several, finally hiring a Chinese man.

Woody immediately became suspicious, claiming there was no such thing in America as a Chinese gardener. "He looks Japanese to me," he contended.

I disagreed.

He said, "As a Chinaman yourself, you should know a fellow countryman, but I'm still suspicious of this fellow."

I assured him that he had no reason to be. But he was persistent, and told me to send him in for questioning.

The Chinese gardener appeared. His name was Fu Chu Lu. He had an accent.

Woody began, "Repeat after me, Mr. Lu: 'I have a 1940 Ford.'"

The gardener said, "I have a nineteen florty Flord."

"Do Chinese people in China eat chop suey?"

"No."

"How do you wash woolen socks?"

"In clold water."

Woody patted him on the back. The Chinese grinned. "Get

back to work," Woody said. The gardener bowed and left. Turning to me, Woody stated, "I have adjudicated the validity of his claim. That fellow is a true son of the dragon."

I can only speculate how Woody might have reacted today to astronauts exploring the mysteries of the universe. One night, strolling arm in arm around the estate, we saw a falling star. I said to him, "Make a wish."

He said he did.

A few moments later, and in a romantic mood, I proposed we break the traditional rules of the game and reveal our wishes. He agreed, and asked what mine was.

"To love you forever," I said, and I believe I blushed slightly. Then I asked, "What was yours?" hoping it would be something equally romantic.

"My wish was that no fragment of the star would fall into my martini."

I heard John Decker pose him the question, "Do you think there's intelligent life on any of the planets?"

Woody's answer was, "There damn well better be, because there's none on this one."

I believe our romance officially ended the night a quartet was singing "You Tell Me Your Dream and I'll Tell You Mine" on the radio—to me a beautiful oldtime standard—and he started yelling, "Turn off that accursed quartet!"

I silenced the machine, and wondered aloud, "What do you dream about, Woody?" half expecting him to whisper "You."

Instead, he raved, "They're always chasing me in my dreams —doctors, lawyers, pregnant women, affirming the charge that I was to blame for their swollen abdomens."

"Accept it as a compliment," I suggested.

"Maybe at my age I should," he said.

Woody chose to ignore tragedy . . . to look the other way. He did, however, attend funerals of close friends, and on these mournful occasions he saw to it that his car was well stocked with potables to assuage his grieving.

We encountered an unexpected turn of events at the 1942 funeral of John Barrymore—it could be considered humorous, if comedy and death can be linked together.

Woody and I were riding in a cavalcade of cars bound for the cemetery, and we passed through the Mexican quarter of Los Angeles. There was a traffic snarl, necessitating a dead stop. Instantly Woody was recognized by some street loiterers who rushed the car with cries of "¡Viva W.C. Fields!" and "¡Ay, Caramba!" He was startled, but, recovering his composure, handed one of them a cocktail shaker filled with martinis and instructed, "Have a drink for good old Jack Barrymore."

At least six of them took a drink before the funeral procession started up again and each one toasted "To good old Jack!"

Woody laughed and said, "That's the way he would have wanted it."

He had no inkling that tragedy would occur on his own grounds. One afternoon he was sitting in an upstairs room sweeping his estate with a powerful telescope thrust out of an open window. He was looking for his usual "marauding bands of savages."

Into focus came a party of men running at top speed. His first impulse, he told me afterward, was to hoist a white flag of surrender. As he always said, "If outnumbered, don't fight 'em—think of a way to screw 'em." Closer scrutiny disclosed that the group of men was heading for his cement-bottomed lily pond. Soon he saw them lift the wet, inert body of a child from its waters.

The child was Christopher, the two-year-old son of Anthony Quinn and Catherine De Mille, daughter of Cecil B. De Mille. Resuscitation efforts failed to revive the boy.

Woody withdrew from the window and after much contemplation and head shaking, sought solace in drink. For hours he was depressed.

In the morning he issued a command to the servants: "Drain that dratted pond."

Fifteen

WOODY drove any number of people nearly crazy, almost to the point of running screaming into the night or telephoning the nearest insane asylum and demanding to be committed. He had the knack. Whether he employed these tactics through the motivation of sadism or for comedic reasons, I couldn't comprehend. So well could he conceal his true emotions that it was impossible to penetrate to the truth. Many have called him a simple human being. I disagree. No actor—especially one from his lonesome, poverty-ridden youth—can be characterized as simple.

Fields enjoyed personally sending his own telegrams. He disliked doing so by telephone or having a servant take them to Western Union for him. "Never deal with a middleman if possible," was his credo. He would drive to Hollywood, where the same woman struggled with his wires for a number of years. Each time I saw her she seemed to have aged perceptibly. I cannot categorically state that this was caused by irritation and frustration from dealing with Woody, but I can say that he didn't exactly have a Fountain of Youth effect on her.

The Western Union operator—whom I shall call Miss

Genevieve Purcell—instantly recognized the comedian upon his initial visit to the office, but kept up the pretense of anonymity that he desired when he signed wires with "Claude Nesselrode," "Oglethorpe P. Bushwacker," and other aliases.

On the first visit Miss Purcell played it straight when she asked for his address.

"2015 De Mille Drive," he said.

"I thought Mr. W.C. Fields lived there," she said.

"He does," Woody said. "I'm his chef."

Often when the actor dispatched a long, rambling wire, Miss Purcell tried to be helpful by suggesting that he use one word instead of two in a number of places. Woody would have none of it, despite her pointing out how much money he would save.

"My good woman," he said, "I appreciate the fact that you are perhaps the only person on the face of the earth who has tried to save me a handful of coppers. However, I wish no deletion of my literary gems."

On only one occasion did Miss Purcell speak her mind. She pointed her forefinger at one of his phrases. "I wouldn't call this sentence a literary gem," was her opinion. "It is flawed by grammatical errors."

"Those are not errors," Woody said, defending his prose. "They are either flyspecks, or I've used the English archaic vernacular."

A recurring discussion with Miss Purcell was over the yellow paper used by her company. "It's too bad you knocked Postal Telegraph out of business," he said, recalling Western Union's former competitor. "They used a baby-blue colored paper that had a soothing effect, no matter how tragic the message. If a man received a wire in the dead of night that read 'We regret to inform you of the death of your loving wife, Agnes P. Osawatomie,' the shock wasn't too bad. But if the same news came on *your* frightening paper, the husband might reach for the arsenic."

He went so far as to bring his own stationery with a huge
W.C. FIELDS imprinted at the top and tried to induce Miss
Purcell to send a wire on it.

Miss Purcell was constantly striving to be helpful—such as
the day Woody handed her a wire that was to get him out of
a dinner invitation that he had accepted:

"Mr. Fields regrets he is unable to attend your dinner due
to a severe case of triple pneumonia he has contracted from
the bite of a flowering dogwood."

For once he sought Miss Purcell's advice, wondering if she
considered the telegram convincing.

The operator shook her head. "Frankly, Mr. Fields, it doesn't
make sense. I've never heard of triple pneumonia, and besides,
no one ever caught a virus from a flower; and furthermore,
a flower doesn't bite."

"Hmmm," Woody debated, and then asked, "What about
snapdragons?"

Miss Purcell appeared startled. But before she could answer,
he asked, "Did the telegram confuse you?"

"It certainly did," she confessed.

He rubbed his hands together in delight. "Good. Excellent.
Send it as is. That was the original purpose."

Once Miss Purcell actually complimented him on a wire.
It was to Dave Chasen:

*Dear David, Last night I drank one of your steaks. It was too
tender to chew on. God how I enjoyed it. I want to thank you
for your thoughtfulness and for the delicious food. Sincerely
and always your friend,*

Bill Fields

"Lovely composition," Miss Purcell purred.

"It's nice to know that a big company appreciates an outsider,"
Fields said.

If he refused to omit words to save money, he had a

compensatory trick of deliberately running words together to cut costs. Miss Purcell never failed to catch him at this. He told me it worked in foreign countries, especially in the Orient, where he could combine any number of words he pleased, such as: "Willmeetyouatfiveoclockwednesdaymorning."

"But wasn't it hard on persons receiving the wires?" I asked him.

"Certainly," he returned. "Particularly if they'd had a few snorts. But it had its advantages. The Women's Temperance Union in Lower Mongolia gave me a plaque for managing to sober up a lot of people."

Competent telephone operators were difficult to obtain during wartime, and I don't think W.C. Fields, the terror of the wires, made it any easier.

One of his favorite tricks was to dial the long distance operator and place a person-to-person call to Otto P. O'Sneed, Jr., in New York City. The operator, after contacting New York City Information, informed Woody that no Otto P. O'Sneed, Jr. could be located, and did he have a street address for him?

"Certainly not," Woody would reply. "None is necessary," and he would explain why, with some extravagant tall tale such as, "Mr. O'Sneed is world famous . . . the toast of Broadway . . . including both upper and lower, I might add. He was the first man in the world with asthma to whistle 'I'm Forever Blowing Bubbles' while upside down in a keg of lager beer."

Each week he had a new name, plus some extraordinary feat the man he wished to speak with had accomplished.

Another of his gags was to ask Information for the number of John Smith. Of course there was a multiplicity of John Smiths, and the operator had been trained not to give out more than three numbers for a common name. When the hapless girl asked for a street address, Woody had none, but would start to *describe* Mr. Smith:

"Operator, Mr. Smith should be easy to locate. He has anthropoidal arms and a peanut-sized head. His body appears to be shaggy, but it's deceiving in the winter because of a moth-eaten overcoat he wears. He's . . ."

At this juncture the operator usually said, "I'm sorry, sir, I am unable to help you,"—and perhaps rushed to the supervisor.

Then there was the time Woody misplaced Jack Barrymore's unlisted number. Now, if there is anything the telephone company protects, it's the privacy of an unlisted number. "I'm sorry, sir, but we can give out the number only in case of a dire emergency," Woody was told.

"I fully understand," he politely returned, "but this *is* an emergency."

"Could you state the nature of the emergency?" the chief operator asked.

"Locked bowels," Woody answered. "Is that dire enough?"

I once heard him ask for the number of Cletus Z. Cornpone, and when the operator wanted to know how to spell the name, he said: " 'C' as in cornucopia, 'O' as in omnivorous, 'R' as in rucksack, 'N' as in neolithic, 'P' as in pneumatoscopic, 'O' as in onslaught, 'N' as in nihility, and 'E' as in eiderdown."

By the time he concluded, the poor operator's head must have been in a whirl, but I always surmised that if she snapped out of it with her sanity intact, her vocabulary would have been sure to improve.

Once when he spoke with his customary hoarseness and nasality, an operator who was presumably new and as yet not broken in to the set policies of the company, said, "Pardon me, sir, I can hardly understand you because you're talking just like W.C. Fields."

When Woody's telephone bill would arrive around the middle of the month he usually took a cursory glance at the amount and instructed either his secretary or me to make out a check for the amount. The monthly bill could be around $121.95 including tax on a number of long-distance calls—but he made no complaint of these; what did bother him was a call to Sherman Oaks in the San Fernando Valley. Known as a unit call, it totaled about nine cents.

"Get an itemized bill from the company," he instructed, "and find out the Sherman Oaks number that was called. Someone is taking advantage of me."

Just to annoy the operator he would crunch celery while trying to get a number from Information. Another ploy was a rising paroxysm of coughing that would increase in volume while he was asking Information for the number of Olive View Sanitarium, a local hospital for lung patients.

Woody once said, "If anyone turns over in his grave it's because the undertaker sold him a lopsided casket." He was ahead of his time when he would jokingly complain about the high cost of dying. His pet name for undertakers was "embalming fluid squirters." The price of caskets upset him.

"If the deceased would travel anywhere in them, the price would be right," he maintained, "but if you're just to rot in the ground and wait for the maggots, what they charge is ridiculous."

After the death of his good friend Sam Hardy, his wrath against funeral directors was fanned into a fury. He constantly bugged one man who headed an internationally-known cemetery by firing questions like: "Can a person furnish his own casket? Would a large radio cabinet be acceptable for burial if hollowed out and made into a child's casket? My uncle, a midget, is dying; can I get a special rate for him? Can I bury a dog in his own doghouse? Is it permitted to plant tomatoes atop the grave? If I own a funeral plot, am I allowed to dig there for fishing worms after a rain? Is there any way the deceased can signal after interment if he's still alive? How do I know you're not going to dig up the casket after a funeral and re-sell it?"

Speaking of death, I overheard him say, "I'd sooner be dead in Los Angeles than alive in Philadelphia." During a discussion of which business had the most headaches, he proclaimed: "Undertaking in Philadelphia. A mortician can hardly tell if he's burying a dead person or a live one."

I believe he nudged his favorite funeral director a step closer to his own grave when he launched into a dissertation on methods of body disposal in Tibet—he claimed to have traveled extensively there while studying the doctrine of Gautama Buddha in a convent, under a Buddhist priest.

"Those learned people," Woody told the funeral director, "either feed bodies to the birds, which are mostly vultures, or the animals, or just cast them into the rivers. Now, just suppose I started a campaign here to abolish cemeteries and follow the Tibetan customs. Where would you and your organization be?"

He generally hung up the telephone while the funeral director was still sputtering.

Of studio property men, he said: "Property men are masters of organized bungling. They all took a mail-order course, failed to pass the examinations, and bought false diplomas. Only in hitchhiking would they excel, due to their abnormally long, flat thumbs that got that way when the hammers they wielded missed nails."

I suppose he did have some legitimate cause for complaint, for I know of five separate occasions when prop men caused him untold anguish. Once, with three hungry lionesses in close pursuit, he reached his escape exit—only to find the door nailed shut. "They would have devoured me," Woody stated, "but I had just taken a drink and all three were members of the Women's Christian Temperance Union."

In a war picture a property man set off a bomb—by mistake, of course, but Woody believed the worst, and a studio doctor had to probe his leg for assorted pieces of scrap metal. Another prop man started a truck unexpectedly when Woody was in it, and the sudden jerking fractured a vertebra in his neck. Then there was that shaving scene where Woody was supposed to have been furnished with a dull razor. It was honed to a fine degree of sharpness, and Woody came out of the scene bleeding as if he'd shoved his face into a lawnmower.

The one time property men really went to his rescue he was overly sarcastic. Ailing, he had to be hoisted into the saddle of a bicycle. Men were standing around to catch him if he fell. Everything worked out nicely, but as he pedaled off the set, he bumped into some scenery and fell to the floor. As several property men pulled him to his feet, he mumbled, "Thanks very much, boys, for catching me on the first bounce."

He always claimed that plumbers were deep-sea divers out of work, who were too stupid to tell you when the water was turned back on again. "There is a national conspiracy among that trade," he stated, "to start banging on pipes when their customers have hangovers of giant proportions.

"They have an uncanny knack of being able to disconnect the water just as you are in the midst of shaving or about to flush the toilet.

"Furthermore, I think they have skeleton keys that will open the doors of most houses, which they sneak into like burglars in the night to purposely clog up the drains. When called in, they bring along what is known as a snake, a long thin, metallic contrivance that probes far down into the pipes to clean them out. Now I'd be happier if these plumbers would only substitute a real snake such as a diamondback rattler, because, due to their abysmal ignorance, they wouldn't know one end of the reptile from the other—and it's easy to realize what the results could be."

One of his most bitter battles was the time he fought and lost the decision to a certain dentist, who must remain nameless. I'll call him Dr. Price, which is a fitting name.

Woody was in great pain one evening, complaining that anything cold he drank touched a raw nerve in his front tooth. As no one ever invented or drank a hot martini, he was in pain most of the night. In the morning we took a chance and went to Dr. Price, a dentist recommended by a friend.

"The friend must have been an enemy," Woody commented later.

Dr. Price extracted the tooth and put in a false one.

Woody wanted to pay him cash for the work, which might have come to a hundred or a hundred twenty-five dollars.

Dr. Price was most gracious. "I'll bill you later," he said. "Don't worry about it."

The bill arrived so speedily that Woody claimed it was delivered by courier and that we "just beat it home by ten minutes."

The bill "for services rendered" by Dr. Price was for twelve hundred dollars.

The moment his eyes fell on the amount he let out a yell that echoed through the house and brought several servants on the run. "It's calamitous!" he yelped. "Astronomical! Ruinous! Brigandry! Not only that, but by God, it's too high!"

Woody raved like a man gone berserk. "Dentists, lawyers, doctors," he shouted, "are all a bunch of thieving bastards. These goddamned professional men turn into professional thieves sooner or later. The first two months after they get their license they want to save humanity; after that they destroy it and only want to save money. They can hold you up better with a pen than Jesse James could with a gun, and for far larger sums than were ever taken from a stagecoach."

Naturally he went to court, and I went along to calm him and keep him from being held in contempt. His lawyer carefully coached him on what to say on the witness stand, but he cast the advice aside in the same manner he did with all his comedy scripts.

"I didn't really need the false tooth," he stated. "Chewing meat isn't important to me."

The dentist's lawyer asked what he considered important to chew, and the answer was, "Only olives or pearl onions."

Under oath, Woody admitted that he had made an irretrievable mistake: He should have bitten the dentist's fingers off so he couldn't have made out the bill. Roaring laughter filled the courtroom, and the judge reprimanded the plaintiff and threatened to clear the room of spectators.

The outcome was that he lost the case. "The judge must have been a dentist in disguise," he complained on the way home.

A year later he needed a cavity filled and said he was going to let either the chauffeur, gardener, or butler do it, that no dentist was getting a second chance to rob him.

I knew of a dentist who doubled as a pilot for Western Airlines, a Dr. Edward K. Hertford, who was a friend of my sister, Eloise. Eventually he was to give up flying and open a full-time dentistry practice in Burbank. I induced Woody to make an appointment with him.

At first Woody was distrustful of Dr. Hertford, unable to dim the bitter memories of his $1,200 tooth. When he received Dr. Hertford's bill, a nominal one, he remarked to me, "Chinaman, that young dentist is superb. A marvelous technician."

From then on they became the best of friends. The doctor wanted nothing from Woody but friendship. Woody was often the last patient of the day, and stayed for dinner. So fond was Dr. Hertford of the actor that through the years he has sentimentally saved a half-empty bottle of gin and one of vermouth that Woody brought over to his house. He has been known occasionally to dig into his files for the W.C. Fields X-rays and regard them fondly.

Woody's eating habits at restaurants intrigued the dentist. After ordering an enormous meal, the actor picked at it like a canary.

Dr. Hertford asked him why he didn't have just a salad or a sandwich.

"I just want to give the dishwashers and bus boys a little work," he explained. "They get soft and lazy on small orders."

Earl Carroll called up Woody and invited him and others he might care to bring to a dinner for the five men who had a hand in the laying-of-the-cornerstone ceremonies of the Earl Carroll Theatre. Woody was one of them, along with Jack Benny and a trio of actors I have forgotten.

Woody pressed a hundred-dollar bill into Dr. Hertford's hand as we drove to the theatre. "Now, Eddie, take it and don't argue," he ordered. "You're my guest, but I want you to pay the bill. This cheap sonofabitch Earl Carroll wouldn't invite us to have dinner and drinks. It's just dinner. So we'll get a bill for the liquid refreshment. You pay it out of this."

Earlier that evening he had repeatedly told Dr. Hertford and me how awful he felt. His facial coloring was unhealthy.

Expected to do a number, he had brought along a special hat and carried his cane. At the table he began his round of martinis. His face seemed to be turning a sickly green.

Then the spotlight focused on him, and the light acted like a shot of adrenalin. Bouncing from the chair, he jogged to the stairs, climbed nimbly to the stage, and performed flawless pantomime. He got a big hand.

Back at the table, they cut off the spotlight, and Woody practically collapsed into the chair. "Chinaman . . . Eddie . . ." he said weakly, "Let's get out of here." He could hardly make it to the car. He was quite ill that night, but for the few minutes he had been "on," his troubles seemed to have disappeared.

Dr. Hertford was dining with us one evening (I had first coached him about punctuality and early departure), and as we were having coffee in the living room the telephone rang. It was Sam Goldwyn.

I heard Woody say, "Yes . . . yes, Sam. Good idea, Sam. Love to, Sam. Yeah, Sam. Happy to oblige you, Sam." There was a pause while Goldwyn said something, and then Woody continued, "I know, Sam. A worthy cause. Any charity is. No question about it. Especially this one. But there's my salary to consider, Sam. How much do I get? Fifty-five hundred a day is my standard rate, Sam, nothing less."

By this time Goldwyn began shouting and we had no trouble overhearing him cry, "I'll call you back," and he hung up.

"He'll never call," Woody predicted—and he never did.

On another occasion when Dr. Hertford paid him a social call, Woody decided to visit the liquor storage room for an after-dinner bottle of brandy and benedictine. As he walked away twirling a key ring containing over fifty keys, he kept glancing over his shoulder, using the excuse, "Have to be careful of brigands, you know."

He was gone for over fifteen minutes. I told Dr. Hertford, "It doesn't take that long for him to find a bottle of liquor. Something must be wrong."

Something certainly was. He had put a lock on the inside— one requiring a key—and had locked himself in. Since he was slightly befuddled from drinking, selection of the right key became a major production.

He shouted instructions to me through the door. "Get the fire department and have them run a ladder up to the window." I started for the telephone, when I heard him call, "Tell them not to hurry. I'm quite comfortable in here, surrounded by my friends."

Dr. Hertford told Woody his teeth were in better condition than those of most men in his age bracket and said he had what dentists call "a good mouth."

The compliment delighted him: "My teeth are well preserved, due to alcohol." In a jocular mood, he stated, "I need good teeth so I can draw my upper lip back and snarl. It scares children and keeps them at a safe distance."

Although Woody knew that Dr. Hertford was an airline pilot, he repeatedly mentioned how he wouldn't trust or have faith in any airplane that was ever built. It was his opinion that "It's the mechanics who cause most of the major accidents. They're notoriously poor drinkers, and those who come to work with hangovers can easily forget to tighten a certain important nut or bolt. The newspapers always say the same thing: 'Cause of crash unknown.'" He continued his tirade against aviation by asserting: "I don't even trust a bird to be able to find south during wintertime, and I wouldn't feel safe with any pilot—even if his name were Wright and he had a brother."

Later he altered the statement by saying that he would feel perfectly comfortable with Dr. Hertford. He said he didn't want to fly with anyone else. He knew his friend's route was to San Francisco, Palm Springs, San Diego, and around the Imperial Valley, but he kept insisting that he fly him to New York. Even after the pilot explained the rules and regulations, Woody didn't give up.

"Maybe I can talk you into it, once I get aboard," he suggested slyly.

Knowing that Woody had been rated as the greatest juggler in the world, and rightfully so, Dr. Hertford once asked him if he would display a little of his abilities.

"Eddie," Woody said seriously, "I'd do it in a second, but my hands are so stiff I couldn't even get started."

He became saddened. Later he recollected, "I could juggle anything in my day. Balls, cigar boxes, knives . . . But there was one thing I could never juggle."

I asked what it was.

"My income tax," he said.

Dr. Hertford asked how it felt to be recognized as the number one juggler in the world and to think that no man was superior.

"Believe me, it isn't worth the effort," Woody answered. In the same serious vein he said, "To be a comedian is one of the saddest things in life."

During World War II, Dr. Hertford wrote Woody a letter from Alaska where he was flying. In it he commented, "It's hard to go to the bathroom here because I can't find 'it' in this freezing weather."

Woody answered, "Don't worry, son, I haven't found mine in forty years."

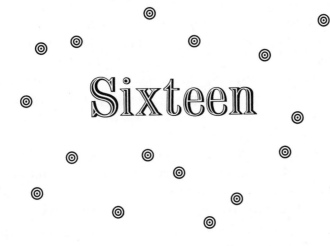

Sixteen

WHEN Woody made his last few movies, he no longer kept his drinks in his dressing room, but out in the open: A coffee pot, holding cracked ice heavily laced with gin, rested on a hot plate.

Someone came along, and thinking it was coffee, snapped on the switch. "You preposterous fool!" Woody screamed, "Do you want to blow us all up? What I have in this pot is highly volatile."

He was not in the best of humor that day, as was evidenced when he sat twirling an old prop watch. A dignified female member of the cast commented, "Very unusual watch you have, Mr. Fields."

"Ah, yes," Woody replied, explaining that it was tossed to him from the Royal Box by the King of Spain.

The woman placed a hand over her ear, and bending her head forward, said, "Did you say the King of Spades?"

In a fairly loud aside, Woody commented to me, "I'd like to wrap it around her goddamned neck," and he bellowed, "The King of Spain!"

His ill-tempered humor seemed to desert him temporarily

when he was approached by director Andrew L. Stone to do a skit in the *Sensations of 1945*. Stone gave him carte blanche and said he could pick any skit he wanted. He was to receive $25,000.

He chose one about riding in a train, arriving in a compartment filled to overflowing with liquor bottles. But the scene was no good; his timing was way off. Mr. Stone consulted Woody's agent, Charley Beyer.

"I've got to take it out," he said, "it's really very bad."

Beyer smelled trouble, shrugged, and said he would talk with Woody. To his surprise, Woody was very upset and confounded him by saying, "I don't want him paying me twenty-five grand and not getting his money's worth. I'll go back and do anything else that Andy wants me to do."

He did another skit, and in a way, humbled himself by doing the work of a stooge, thus prompting Mr. Stone to remark, "I have never met a more charming and gracious man and one so easy to work with."

But his condition was gradually deteriorating. As the year changed to 1946, he ate sparingly, slept fitfully, and drank increasingly. At night he was so restless that I had boards placed around his bed to keep him from sleepwalking—although it was hard to detect if he were actually sleepwalking or bound for a portable bar. I told him he was the only person in the world who had the distinction of being able to mix a martini in his sleep.

He had alcoholic cirrhosis of the liver. His abdomen began to swell and fill with water, distending his stomach. Slowly he lost the muscular strength of his arms and legs, and they became spidery in appearance, with a wilted look.

Also, his kidneys were malfunctioning.

When a doctor informed him his stomach was waterlogged, he moaned, "God forbid! I always knew that abominable, tasteless liquid would some day poison me."

His breathing was becoming difficult, and I could detect a

profound general weakness enveloping him. The palms of his hands had reddish blotches, his face was noticeably paling, and tiny veins appeared on his chest and around the collar bone. The sight of him sent twisting daggers of sorrow into my heart.

He had a premonition of death. The only question in his mind was: How soon? "The old Reaper's coming to get me, Chinaman," he kept repeating.

The lease on the house was expiring, and he told me and his secretary that he wasn't going to renew it. To do so would have entailed much bartering and bickering with the landlord —something that he would have loved in the old days. But he realized that a fight now over mere prices was far too debilitating for him.

Announcing in a doomed voice that he was going to the Las Encinas Sanitarium in Pasadena, he sent the household effects to storage and dismissed his last two servants. Then, one dark, rain-threatening day he said to me, "Take my arm, Chinaman, and let's walk around the grounds."

I took his arm and he leaned heavily on me for support. He inspected everything—particularly the flowers. "It's too bad their lives are so short," he said, half aloud.

He took one sweeping farewell look, his head slowly swiveling to encompass the entire grounds. In his eyes I detected resigned acceptance that this was the final time he would view the estate he loved. He had spent seven years here, his longest tenure in any one place.

It began to rain the heavy, semi-tropical drops that sometimes pelt down in southern California and by the time we reached the car that would carry us to the sanitarium, it was coming down in heavy sheets.

"The gods are against me," he muttered after a loud crack of thunder, and I reached for his hand and held it tightly as we drove away.

He lowered his head, chin touching his chest, and closed his eyes, remaining in that position for a full ten minutes. I believe that he was crying and didn't want me to know.

He paid $500 a week for his private bungalow, $65 for my small adjoining room, plus additional sums for 'round-the-clock private nurses.

At Las Encinas I waited on him hand and foot, kept encouraging him to fight to live, read to him, reminisced, did *petit point* work, and watered down his liquor. I would open a bottle of gin, pour about a third of it down the drain, and add water. He was in no condition to notice the difference.

For a few weeks I got away with this until the day he offered Bob Howard a drink.

Howard made a wry face. "Boy, this is weak," he said distastefully.

Reaching for the bottle, Woody sniffed the contents. "It's the work of that infernal Chinaman," he said. "They're a very devious race."

Of course I denied the charge.

I had to go to town on an errand, and upon returning found all my clothes out on the lawn. Later I learned that Woody had bribed an attendant to do this. I calmly gathered them up and hung them back in my closet, with a solemn promise to Woody that I would never again tamper with his liquor bottles.

Days when I was tired, bored, or when he was sleeping, I wandered around the lovely landscaped surroundings. There was a fresh, earthy smell to the grounds. But inside the bungalow there was also an odor—the odor of death. It hung in the air. You could almost touch it.

At night, if warm, we sat in front of the cottage. The view was pretty, with soft, green lawns and tall stately trees. One of those nights I saw him pulling at his fingers. He said, "I'm taking all the jewelry off my fingers . . . hear it click . . . hear it click. It's falling in the bucket. I want you to take the bucket and open a little jewelry shop."

I tried gently to tell him that there wasn't any jewelry, that he was imagining it, like a dream, but I couldn't convince him. He got angry and called me a liar, and claimed I just wanted to give him an argument.

"You're lazy and don't want to open up a store," he said. "I tried to give you a house and you refused, and I tried to give you a restaurant because you're such a good cook and again you refused."

He suffered from the recurrent hallucination that he was going to put me in business. His thoughts were disconnected. "I'm going to give you one bottle of every kind of liquor that exists," he would say, "and a small jigger. You pour the customers a drink from the small jigger and that way you'll make money."

It was pitiful to hear him talk that way.

During his sickness I kept arguing with his friends, begging them not to bring him liquor. With the medication he was taking, it was both torturous and dangerous for him to drink. Despite my precautions, his devoted followers still smuggled in the bottles. Now, in retrospect, I see it didn't really matter so much.

The bungalow had no air conditioning, only an overhead fan. On hot days I would take a hose and water the roof at nap time. He would imagine he was listening to the rain and it had the same soothing effect. At a certain hour I would say, "It's rainmaking time," and he would say, "What would I do without my little Chinaman?"

Intermittently his spirit soared and briefly he was the old W.C. Fields again. One day his doctor called to see him, the medic's pocket bulging with fountain pens and thermometers. After a cursory examination, he started for the door, but Woody stopped him.

"Just a moment, Doctor."

The physician halted and turned around. "Yes, Mr. Fields?"

"How are your bowels?"

On Christmas Day, shortly before noon, he said to me, "Grab everything and run. The vultures are coming."

At three minutes past noon he called weakly, "Chinaman." I took his hand tenderly and bent low over the bed. His fingers tightened around mine. They felt dry, scaly, lifeless.

"Goddamn it!" he cursed forcefully, his face twisted with pain, and then his voice trailed away.

"Woody, Woody, Woody," was all I could say.

"Goddamn," he repeated, and his eyes opened wider than I'd ever seen them. His voice was the rustling and crackling of dry leaves. "Goddamn the whole friggin' world and everyone in it but you, Carlotta."

Those were his last words. He was shaken by a violent stomach hemorrhage. Moments later he was dead, at the age of sixty-eight.

The doctor came in, examined him, and stated, "Well, it's all over."

"What do I do with the bed?" the nurse asked me.

I told her to have it and the mattress cleaned and that I would send for it. I had bought him that bed because he wouldn't buy a decent one for himself.

Not having been informed, the owner of the sanitarium came to pay a visit. He was unaware of the death. "Merry Christmas, everyone!" he greeted.

Neither did Bill Grady nor Dave Chasen know of the passing of their comedian friend. They were arriving at Las Encinas just about the time I was following Woody's body on a black hearse on its way to the mortuary. His two old friends had brought along a hamper containing some fine steaks and bottles of rare old bourbon. They had planned to cook the steaks in the kitchenette. Both were wearing red jackets, and wanting to give Woody a laugh, they dropped to their hands and knees, planning to walk into the room in the guise of midgets.

They knocked, and waited. A nurse opened the door, looked down at them, and said, "Mr. Fields died an hour ago."

Unsteadily they got up and went inside, opened one of the bottles of whisky, took stiff drinks, and left the steaks. Then they drove to Chasen's restaurant, where they were joined by a group of Woody's friends which included Ben Hecht, Eddie Sutherland, Grantland Rice, Greg La Cava, and Gene Fowler.

Underneath a brilliant work of art—John Decker's painting of Woody as Queen Victoria—they clinked glasses, toasted him, and reminisced. After the last regular restaurant customer departed, Chasen locked the door, and the drinking continued unabated throughout the night.

It was pouring rain. All present agreed it was exactly the kind of night that Bill Fields . . . or "Uncle Willie" . . . or "Uncle Claude" . . . or, as I called him, Woody, would have loved.

That day, comedian Bob Hope, who had not yet heard the tragic news, quipped about Fields' bibulous proclivities during his part of a two-hour, all-star radio broadcast. When apprised of the comedian's death, he said, "The world certainly is going to lose a lot of laughs."

The bungalow at Las Encinas was immediately impounded. I even lost my clothes and *petit point* work. Mrs. Harriet V. Fields and her son, Claude—neither of whom had seen Woody for an indeterminate number of years—arrived to take charge of the effects and funeral arrangements.

There was a stipulation in his will that he be immediately cremated and that there be no funeral of any kind. Woody had always said to me, "I don't want any funeral. Just cremate me. I had enough of the cold ground in my youth."

But for the man who expressly stated he desired no funeral, there were three. The first, a non-sectarian one, was well attended. Edgar Bergen delivered the eulogy. The parts of it that I can remember, with the help of Mr. Bergen, were:

"We are uninvited guests here, you know, because Bill didn't want a religious funeral service. He said to me once,

'If I ever found a church that didn't believe in knocking all the other churches, I might consider joining it.'

"Ministers around the world will find sermons from Bill's life, but they will never enjoy one-tenth of his popularity.

"He had the genius of comedy, but also the courage to say what he felt and thought about religion.

"On the way to the funeral I saw a sign on a mountainside: *JESUS CHRIST SAVES SINNERS*. If this is true, Bill has qualified, for he has sinned. Yet if it isn't true, he would want no part of false advertising, because he always insisted on giving you your money's worth at the box-office.

"It seems wrong not to pray for a man who gave such happiness to the world. But that was the way he wanted it.

"Bill knew life, and knew that laughter was the way to live it. He knew that happiness depended on disposition, not position.

"We simply say, Farewell."

After this first funeral, Mrs. Fields had another one—this time a Catholic ceremony.

When the Fields family departed, I tried to go to the crypt, but was stopped by a cemetery official who said, "On orders of the Fields family, you are not to be admitted until the crypt is sealed."

I felt shut out completely from the man I had loved.

After the crypt was sealed, I entered the room with the Reverend Mae Taylor, a leading Hollywood practitioner. We approached the crypt, and held a third funeral with the Reverend Taylor presiding.

For four years there was bitter strife among the claimants to share in the W.C. Fields estate. In his will, the bulk of the estate was to go for the establishment of an orphanage. Lawyers knocked out this provision.

Woody's wife and son became the major beneficiaries.

In court a letter was read that Fields had written to his wife in 1932, and signed "Claude":

"I note the derogatory rumors concerning my use of

alcoholic stimulants and lavish living. It is the penalty of greatness. I would have sworn when these rumors reached you, you would have retaliated as did Lincoln when some nosey parker said that Grant was continually in his cups. 'Find out the brand of whisky he drinks and send a barrel to each of my generals,' Lincoln replied. For Grant was making good, and I have made good as far as you are concerned, for as long as I have known you I have never failed you with the bacon."

I was instrumental in getting Woody's illegitimate son a $10,000 share of the estate.

I received $50 weekly for ten years.

The first half-dozen years after Woody's demise weighed on me heavily as I changed my standard of living, going from job to job, until I finally landed one at Technicolor Incorporated, where I am presently employed. For recreation on weekends I paint in pastels and oils.

In the settlement of the Fields estate, I received his 1938 Cadillac, a bit of memorabilia I still possess. Regrettably, an important adjunct to the car was missing—his portable bar. Without it the car seemed empty, for the bar was a distinctive touch of Woody's personality and something very sentimental to me. For memories I drive Woody's old Cadillac along the streets we used to frequent.

If I were clairvoyant I am sure that coming from that spacious rear seat, I would still hear that lovable, unmelodious, nasal voice mutter, "Carlotta, my dusky beauty, please employ your skillful touch to concoct another of your delicious martinis."

I only wish I could.

Index